From Spare Room to Superhost:

Mastering Airbnb's platform

Maxwell Rivers

Introduction

Have you ever found yourself walking past that empty spare room, feeling saddened at its wasted potential? Or perhaps, as part of the Airbnb community, but struggling to reach success as desired? If any of this sounds familiar to you, then welcome. You have come to the right place.

Let's consider the issue at hand: For many individuals, becoming an Airbnb host can be both exciting and daunting. On one hand, it offers travelers from around the world an exciting new way of connecting, while sharing unique experiences, earning extra income, and connecting with new people through Airbnb; but on the other hand, it can feel daunting to set up listings, attract guests, provide exceptional hospitality service - especially those new to this platform.

How can Airbnb hosting unlock its full potential and transform that spare room into a profitable, successful venture? The solution lies within "From Spare Room to Superhost: Mastering Airbnb's Platform". Written by an experienced Airbnb host with extensive knowledge of this platform's nuances, this book serves as your roadmap towards success.

But why should you trust me on this journey? Allow me to demonstrate my credibility: as an experienced Airbnb host myself, I understand your struggles: setting up listings, attracting guests and providing top-notch hospitality are just a few challenges I faced as an amateur host when starting from scratch. But success also brought joys: earning Superhost status was thrilling and receiving positive reviews was satisfying, while building a thriving hosting business is what gave me pride.

Now let's talk about the benefits. By following the strategies outlined in this book, not only will you maximize your earning potential on Airbnb but also create unforgettable experiences for your guests. You will discover how to set up your listing for maximum visibility, attract guests with engaging descriptions and photos, and offer hospitality that goes above and beyond expectations.

Let me show you the proof. In these pages of this book, you'll find real-life examples, success stories and actionable insights from fellow hosts who have experienced remarkable results through Airbnb hosting. From turning an extra room into a desirable retreat space to turning properties into successful hospitality businesses- the possibilities of Airbnb are limitless!

As your host, my promise to you is this: by the time you reach the last page, you'll have all of the tools, knowledge, and confidence necessary for successful Airbnb hosting. However, time is of the essence; now is an opportune time to take action!

So, what are you waiting for? Dive into this book, absorb its wisdom, and start your Airbnb hosting success journey today. Your guests are eagerly waiting, your space is available, and hosting success awaits. Are you ready to transform your spare room into an Airbnb Superhost haven? Get started right away by turning this spare room into Superhost heaven; your guests...and success await your presence.

Let's delve deeper into each element of Airbnb hosting, and how this book will help you navigate each stage.

Chapter 1: Getting Started: Setting Up Your Airbnb Listing

Welcome to the exciting world of Airbnb hosting! In this comprehensive chapter, we will walk you through each step in setting up and optimizing your listing - whether this is your first experience hosting or you just need help optimizing an existing listing, we cover everything necessary for getting off on the right foot.

Understanding the Airbnb Platform

Before diving into the nitty-gritty of setting up your listing, let's take a moment to familiarize ourselves with the Airbnb platform. Airbnb is an online marketplace that connects travelers with hosts who have accommodations to rent. Founded in 2008, Airbnb has revolutionized the way people travel, offering a wide range of unique and personalized accommodations in destinations around the world. Whether you have a spare room, an entire apartment, or even a unique property like a treehouse or a boat, Airbnb provides a platform for you to showcase your space and connect with potential guests.

Creating Your Account

The first step in setting up your Airbnb listing is to create an account. Visit the Airbnb website or download the mobile app and follow the prompts to sign up. You'll need to provide some basic information about yourself, including your name, email address, and phone number. Once your account is created, you'll be ready to start hosting!

Crafting Your Listing

Now it's time to create your listing. Think of your listing as your space's online storefront—it's the first thing potential guests will see when they're browsing for accommodations. Start by uploading high-quality photos of your space that showcase its unique features and amenities. Be sure to include a detailed description that highlights what makes your space special, whether it's the cozy fireplace, the breathtaking views, or the convenient location. Describe the layout of the space, mention any special features or amenities, and provide information about the neighborhood and nearby attractions. The more detailed and accurate your listing is, the more likely you are to attract the right guests.

Setting Your House Rules

Next, you'll need to set some house rules for your guests to follow during their stay. Consider things like whether smoking or pets are allowed, quiet hours, and any other rules or guidelines you want your guests to be aware of. Setting clear and reasonable house rules will help ensure a positive experience for both you and your guests. You can add house rules directly to your listing, and guests will be required to agree to them before booking.

Pricing Your Space

One of the most important aspects of setting up your Airbnb listing is pricing your space competitively. Take some time to research similar listings in your area to get an idea of what other hosts are charging. Consider factors like the size and location of your space, the amenities you offer, and the demand in your area. Pricing your space appropriately will help attract guests and maximize your earnings. Keep in mind that Airbnb charges a service fee to guests, so factor that into your pricing strategy as well.

Providing Amenities

Finally, consider the amenities you'll provide for your guests during their stay. This could include essentials like linens, towels, and toiletries, as well as extras like coffee, tea, and snacks. Think about what will make your guests feel comfortable and at home and be sure to highlight these amenities in your listing. You can also offer additional amenities like Wi-Fi, TV services like Roku, Netflix, other streaming services, or a jacuzzi if you have them available. The more amenities you provide, the more attractive your listing will be to potential guests.

Enhancing Your Listing

Once you've set up the basics of your listing, it's time to think about how you can make it even more appealing to guests. Consider adding some personal touches, such as fresh flowers, artwork, or decorative touches that reflect your personality and style. You can also enhance your listing by offering special promotions or discounts for longer stays, or by providing personalized recommendations for things to see and do in the area. A simple binder containing local restaurant or entertainment information becomes a helpful resources for your guest. The goal is to create a welcoming and inviting space that guests will be excited to book.

Optimizing Your Listing for Search

Now that your listing is set up, it's important to optimize it for search engines to ensure potential guests can find it. Use relevant keywords in your listing title and description to help your listing appear in search results for relevant queries. You can also use the Airbnb search filters to narrow down your target audience based on factors like location, price, and amenities. The more relevant your listing is to a potential guest's search criteria, the more likely they are to book.

Managing Your Calendar

Once your listing is live, it's important to keep your calendar up to date to reflect your availability. Use the Airbnb calendar tool to mark dates when your space is available for booking and dates when it's not. You can also set minimum and maximum stay requirements, as well as adjust your pricing based on demand. Keeping your calendar accurate and up to date will help prevent double bookings and ensure a smooth booking process for you and your guests.

Responding to Inquiries and Bookings

As inquiries and bookings start to come in, it's essential to respond promptly and professionally to potential guests. Be sure to answer any questions they may have about your listing and provide any additional information they request. Once a booking is confirmed, be sure to communicate with your guests leading up to their stay to ensure a smooth check-in process. Providing excellent communication and customer service will help ensure a positive experience for your guests and encourage them to leave positive reviews.

Congratulations! You've successfully set up your Airbnb listing and are well on your way to becoming a successful host. By following the steps outlined in this chapter, you've created a compelling listing that will attract guests and provide them with a memorable experience. Stay tuned for the next chapter, where we'll dive deeper into the world of Airbnb hosting and explore strategies for creating irresistible listings and providing exceptional hospitality. Happy hosting!

Chapter 2: Creating an Irresistible Listing: Tips for Photos and Descriptions

Welcome to Chapter 2 of "From Spare Room to Superhost: Mastering Airbnb's Platform." In this comprehensive guide, we'll delve deeply into the art of creating an irresistible Airbnb listing through the power of stunning photos and captivating descriptions. Your listing serves as the window into your space, inviting potential guests to envision themselves staying there. So, let's explore how to make your listing stand out from the crowd and attract the attention of discerning travelers.

The Importance of High-Quality Photos

Photos are the linchpin of your Airbnb listing. They're the first thing potential guests see when browsing, and they play a crucial role in shaping their perception of your space. High-quality, professional-looking photos can make a significant difference in attracting guests and encouraging them to book. In contrast, poor-quality photos can turn potential guests away, regardless of how wonderful your space may be.

To ensure your photos make a strong impression, follow these essential tips:

Utilize natural light: Natural light is your best friend when it comes to photography. Open curtains and blinds to let in as much natural light as possible, and avoid using harsh overhead lighting or flash, which can create unflattering shadows.

Highlight key features: Capture photos that showcase the most attractive and unique features of your space, whether it's a cozy reading nook, a stunning view, or intricate architectural details. Consider staging the space with tasteful decorations to enhance its appeal further.

Declutter and stage: Before taking photos, declutter and stage your space to make it look its best. Remove any clutter or personal items that might distract from the overall appeal of the space and consider adding decorative touches like fresh flowers or cozy throw blankets to enhance the ambiance.

Use a wide-angle lens: A wide-angle lens can help you capture more of your space in a single shot, making it appear larger and more inviting. If you don't have a wide-angle lens, you can achieve a similar effect by standing in a corner of the room and shooting from a low angle.

Edit carefully: Once you've taken your photos, edit them carefully to enhance their quality and appeal. Use editing software or apps to adjust brightness, contrast, and color balance, but be careful not to overdo it—your photos should look natural and realistic.

By following these tips, you can create a collection of photos that effectively showcase the beauty and uniqueness of your space, enticing potential guests to book their stay.

Crafting Compelling Descriptions

In addition to eye-catching photos, compelling descriptions are essential for capturing the attention of potential guests and convincing them to book your space. Your description is your opportunity to paint a vivid picture of what it's like to stay in your space, highlighting its unique features, amenities, and charm.

Craft a compelling description by considering the following tips:

Be descriptive: Use descriptive language to create a vivid image of your space in the minds of potential guests. Describe the layout of the space, the amenities you offer, and any special features that make your space unique. Use adjectives that evoke a sense of comfort, relaxation, and luxury.

Highlight the benefits: Focus on the benefits of staying in your space, rather than just listing its features. For example, instead of simply mentioning that you have a fully equipped kitchen, emphasize that guests can enjoy the convenience of preparing home-cooked meals during their stay.

Use storytelling techniques: Tell a story about your space and its history or share anecdotes about memorable experiences guests have had there. Personalize your description to give potential guests a sense of the atmosphere and vibe of your space, making them feel more connected to it.

Be honest and transparent: It's essential to be honest and transparent in your description, so guests know exactly what to expect. Be upfront about any quirks or limitations of your space, such as a shared bathroom or noise from nearby construction. Transparency builds trust with potential guests and helps manage their expectations.

Use keywords: Incorporate relevant keywords into your description to improve its visibility in Airbnb search results. Think about the words and phrases potential guests might use when searching for accommodations in your area and include them naturally throughout your description.

By following these tips, you can create a compelling description that effectively communicates the unique appeal of your space and entices potential guests to book their stay.

Engaging Potential Guests with Your Listing

Once you've created stunning photos and compelling descriptions for your Airbnb listing, it's time to engage potential guests and encourage them to book their stay. Here are some additional tips for making your listing irresistible:

Use a catchy title: Your listing title is the first thing potential guests will see, so make it catchy and attention-grabbing. Use descriptive language to highlight the most attractive features of your space and entice guests to click on your listing.

Offer a unique selling proposition: What sets your space apart from the competition? Whether it's a prime location, unique amenities, or exceptional hospitality, be sure to highlight your space's unique selling proposition in your listing. Emphasize what makes your space special and why guests should choose to stay with you.

Include guest reviews: Guest reviews can be a powerful tool for building trust and credibility with potential guests. Include positive reviews from previous guests in your listing to showcase the positive experiences others have had staying in your space. Reviews provide social proof and reassure potential guests that they're making the right choice by booking with you.

Update your listing regularly: Keep your listing fresh and up-to-date by regularly updating your photos, descriptions, and availability. Consider offering seasonal promotions or discounts to attract guests during slower periods. Keeping your listing current and relevant shows potential guests that you're actively engaged and committed to providing an exceptional experience.

Respond promptly to inquiries: Be sure to respond promptly and professionally to inquiries from potential guests. Prompt communication and excellent customer service can help set you apart from the competition and encourage guests to book your space. Be friendly, helpful, and responsive to any questions or concerns potential guests may have and make the booking process as smooth and seamless as possible.

By implementing these strategies, you can create an irresistible Airbnb listing that attracts the attention of potential guests and encourages them to book their stay. Your photos and descriptions serve as the gateway to your space, so invest time and effort into making them as compelling and engaging as possible.

In this chapter, we've explored the importance of high-quality photos and compelling descriptions in creating an irresistible Airbnb listing. Your photos and descriptions are your opportunity to showcase the beauty and uniqueness of your space and entice potential guests to book their stay. By following the tips and strategies outlined in this chapter, you can create a listing that stands out from the crowd and attracts the attention of discerning travelers. Stay tuned for the next chapter, where we'll dive deeper into the world of Airbnb hosting and explore strategies for maximizing your earnings and providing exceptional hospitality.

Chapter 3: Pricing Strategies: Maximizing Your Earnings

Welcome to Chapter 3 of "From Spare Room to Superhost: Mastering Airbnb's Platform." In this extensive guide, we'll delve into the intricate world of pricing strategies on Airbnb and how you can leverage them to maximize your earnings as a host. Pricing your listing effectively is not only about setting the right price but also understanding the nuances of demand, seasonality, and market dynamics. Let's explore in detail the various pricing strategies and techniques you can employ to optimize your earnings on Airbnb.

Understanding the Factors Influencing Pricing

Before we delve into specific pricing strategies, it's crucial to grasp the myriad factors that influence the pricing of your Airbnb listing. Several key elements can significantly impact how much you can charge for your space:

Location: The location of your property plays a pivotal role in determining its value and, consequently, its pricing. Properties situated in prime locations with easy access to attractions, amenities, and public transportation typically command higher prices than those in less desirable areas.

Seasonality: Seasonal fluctuations in demand can have a profound impact on pricing. Properties in popular tourist destinations may experience peak seasons with high demand and peak prices, as well as off-peak seasons with lower demand and consequently lower prices.

Property Type and Amenities: The type of property you offer and the amenities you provide also play a significant role in pricing. Properties with unique features, luxurious amenities, or desirable characteristics (such as a pool or a balcony with a view) may be able to command higher prices than more basic accommodations.

Market Conditions: Local market conditions, including supply and demand dynamics and the competitive landscape, can also affect pricing. It's essential to be aware of market trends and adjust your pricing strategy accordingly to remain competitive and maximize your earnings.

By understanding these factors and how they interplay with each other, you can develop a more nuanced and strategic approach to pricing your Airbnb listing.

Dynamic Pricing Strategies

Dynamic pricing, also known as demand-based pricing or revenue management, is a sophisticated pricing strategy that involves adjusting the price of your listing in real-time based on various factors such as demand, occupancy rates, and market conditions. Dynamic pricing algorithms analyze historical booking data, competitor pricing, and other relevant factors to determine the optimal price for your listing at any given time.

Implementing a dynamic pricing strategy can be highly effective in maximizing your earnings by capitalizing on periods of high demand and adjusting your prices downward during slower periods to attract more bookings. Many third-party pricing tools and software platforms are available to help hosts automate dynamic pricing and optimize their earnings.

When implementing a dynamic pricing strategy, consider the following tips:

Set competitive base rates: Start with a competitive base rate that reflects the value of your space and amenities. This base rate serves as the foundation for your dynamic pricing strategy, with prices fluctuating above or below this baseline based on demand.

Monitor market trends: Keep a close eye on market trends, including local events, holidays, and seasonal fluctuations in demand. Adjust your pricing strategy accordingly to capitalize on periods of high demand and maximize your earnings.

Use data-driven insights: Leverage data-driven insights from dynamic pricing tools and platforms to inform your pricing decisions. Analyze historical booking data, competitor pricing, and other relevant factors to identify trends and opportunities for optimization.

Be flexible: Be prepared to adjust your prices frequently based on changing market conditions and demand patterns. Flexibility is key to maximizing your earnings with dynamic pricing, as it allows you to adapt quickly to changes in the market and stay competitive.

By implementing a dynamic pricing strategy, you can optimize your earnings on Airbnb and maximize the revenue potential of your listing.

Seasonal Pricing Strategies

Seasonal pricing is another effective strategy for maximizing your earnings on Airbnb. Seasonal pricing involves adjusting your prices based on seasonal fluctuations in demand, with higher prices during peak seasons and lower prices during off-peak seasons.

When implementing a seasonal pricing strategy, consider the following tips:

Identify peak and off-peak seasons: Identify the peak and off-peak seasons for your destination based on historical booking data, local events, and seasonal trends. Peak seasons typically coincide with holidays, festivals, and other events that attract tourists, while off-peak seasons are periods of lower demand.

Increase prices during peak seasons: During peak seasons, when demand is high, consider increasing your prices to capitalize on increased demand and maximize your earnings. Consider factors such as local events, holidays, and the availability of competing accommodations when setting your prices.

Offer discounts during off-peak seasons: During off-peak seasons, when demand is lower, consider offering discounts or special promotions to attract guests and fill vacant dates. Offering discounted rates can help you maintain a steady stream of bookings and maximize your occupancy rates during slower periods.

Adjust prices gradually: When adjusting your prices for peak and off-peak seasons, be sure to do so gradually to avoid pricing yourself out of the market or alienating potential guests. Monitor the performance of your listing and adjust your pricing strategy as needed based on guest feedback and booking patterns.

By implementing a seasonal pricing strategy, you can effectively capitalize on seasonal fluctuations in demand and maximize your earnings throughout the year.

Long-Term Pricing Strategies

In addition to dynamic and seasonal pricing strategies, long-term pricing is another important consideration for maximizing your earnings on Airbnb.

Long-term pricing involves offering discounted rates for extended stays, typically ranging from several days to several weeks or months.

When implementing a long-term pricing strategy, consider the following tips:

Offer discounts for extended stays: Consider offering discounted rates for guests who book longer stays, such as weekly or monthly discounts. Offering discounted rates for extended stays can attract guests who are looking for longer-term accommodations and help you maximize your occupancy rates and earnings.

Set minimum stay requirements: Consider setting minimum stay requirements for your listing to encourage longer bookings. For example, you could require a minimum stay of three nights or a week to qualify for discounted rates. Setting minimum stay requirements can help you attract guests who are willing to book longer stays and maximize your earnings.

Be flexible with pricing: Be flexible with your pricing for long-term bookings and willing to negotiate with guests to accommodate their needs. Consider offering flexible cancellation policies and other incentives to attract long-term guests and maximize your occupancy rates and earnings.

By implementing a long-term pricing strategy, you can attract guests who are looking for longer-term accommodations and maximize your earnings by filling vacant dates with extended stays.

In this extensive chapter, we've explored various pricing strategies and techniques for maximizing your earnings on Airbnb. Pricing your space effectively is a multifaceted endeavor that requires a deep understanding of market dynamics, demand patterns, and guest preferences. By leveraging dynamic, seasonal, and long-term pricing strategies, you can optimize your earnings and unlock the full revenue potential of your listing. Remember to stay agile and adaptive, continuously monitoring market trends and adjusting your pricing strategy to stay competitive and maximize your earnings. In the next chapter, we'll delve deeper into the world of Airbnb hosting and explore strategies for providing exceptional hospitality and earning rave reviews from your guests.

Chapter 4: Understanding Guest Expectations: Providing Exceptional Hospitality

Welcome to Chapter 4 of "From Spare Room to Superhost: Mastering Airbnb's Platform." In this extensive chapter, we will delve deeply into the art of understanding guest expectations and providing exceptional hospitality. As a host, your ability to exceed guest expectations can make all the difference in creating memorable experiences and earning rave reviews. We'll explore various aspects of hospitality and strategies you can implement to ensure that every guest leaves your space feeling delighted and satisfied.

The Foundation of Hospitality

Hospitality is not just a service; it's an experience. It's about creating a warm, welcoming environment where guests feel valued, comfortable, and at home. In the realm of Airbnb hosting, hospitality is the cornerstone of success. It's what sets apart ordinary stays from extraordinary ones and transforms guests into loyal advocates for your space.

At its core, hospitality encompasses:

Personalization: Tailoring the guest experience to meet the unique preferences and needs of each guest.

Anticipation: Proactively identifying and addressing guest needs before they arise.

Warmth: Extending genuine warmth and kindness to guests, making them feel valued and appreciated.

Flexibility: Being adaptable and accommodating to guests' requests and preferences.

Attention to detail: Paying meticulous attention to every aspect of the guest experience, from communication to amenities to cleanliness.

By embracing these principles of hospitality, you can create an environment where guests feel welcomed, cared for, and eager to return.

Anticipating Guest Needs

A hallmark of exceptional hospitality is the ability to anticipate and fulfill guest needs before they even realize they have them. By taking proactive steps to anticipate common guest needs, you can enhance the guest experience and demonstrate your commitment to providing exceptional service.

Here are some ways to anticipate guest needs:

Provide clear communication: From the moment a guest makes a booking, ensure that communication is clear, timely, and informative. Provide detailed instructions for check-in, directions to your space, and information about amenities and local attractions. Anticipate any questions or concerns they may have and address them proactively in your communication.

Stock essential amenities: Ensure that your space is stocked with essential amenities such as toiletries, linens, towels, and kitchen basics. Anticipate the needs of your guests by providing thoughtful touches such as coffee, tea, snacks, and bottled water. Consider going the extra mile by providing items that guests may have forgotten to pack, such as phone chargers, umbrellas, or sunscreen.

Offer additional services: Consider offering additional services or amenities to enhance the guest experience. This could include arranging airport transfers, providing grocery delivery services, or offering guided tours of the local area. Anticipate your guests' preferences and interests and tailor your offerings accordingly to provide a personalized and memorable experience.

By anticipating your guests' needs and taking proactive steps to address them, you can create a positive and memorable experience that sets you apart as a superhost.

Creating a Welcoming Atmosphere

Creating a welcoming atmosphere is essential for providing exceptional hospitality and ensuring that your guests feel comfortable and at home during their stay. From the moment your guests arrive, they should feel greeted with warmth and hospitality, setting the tone for a pleasant and enjoyable experience.

Here are some tips for creating a welcoming atmosphere:

Personalize the space: Add personal touches and decorative accents to your space to make it feel warm and inviting. Consider incorporating artwork, fresh flowers, and cozy textiles to create a welcoming ambiance that reflects your personality and style.

Offer a warm welcome: Greet your guests warmly upon their arrival and take the time to show them around your space. Provide them with a brief orientation, pointing out key features and amenities, and answer any questions they may have. Consider leaving a handwritten note or welcome card to make your guests feel appreciated and valued.

Provide a welcome basket: Consider providing your guests with a welcome basket or tray filled with snacks, beverages, and local treats. This thoughtful gesture will make your guests feel welcomed and valued and set the tone for a memorable stay.

Be attentive and responsive: Throughout your guests' stay, be attentive and responsive to their needs. Check in with them periodically to ensure they're comfortable and address any concerns or issues promptly and professionally. Be proactive in anticipating and addressing any potential issues that may arise during their stay.

By creating a welcoming atmosphere and providing attentive and personalized service, you can ensure that your guests feel valued and appreciated during their stay.

Exceeding Guest Expectations

To provide exceptional hospitality and stand out as a superhost, it's essential to go above and beyond to exceed your guests' expectations. By surprising and delighting your guests with unexpected touches and thoughtful gestures, you can create memorable experiences that leave a lasting impression.

Here are some ways to exceed guest expectations:

Provide personalized recommendations: Take the time to get to know your guests and their interests and offer personalized recommendations for things to see and do in the area. Suggest local restaurants, attractions, and activities that align with their preferences and make reservations or arrangements on their behalf if possible. Consider providing a guidebook or map with personalized recommendations to help guests navigate the local area.

Offer special touches: Surprise and delight your guests with special touches and amenities that go above and beyond the ordinary. Consider leaving a handwritten note or welcome card, providing a complimentary bottle of wine or champagne, or arranging for a special celebration or occasion during their stay. Pay attention to the little details that can make a big difference in the guest experience.

Anticipate special occasions: Keep track of special occasions such as birthdays, anniversaries, and milestones, and celebrate them with your guests during their stay. Consider providing a small gift or arranging for a special treat or experience to commemorate the occasion and make it memorable. By going the extra mile to acknowledge and celebrate special occasions, you can create lasting memories for your guests.

Provide exceptional service: Strive to provide exceptional service at every touchpoint of the guest experience, from the initial inquiry to the post-stay follow-up. Be responsive, professional, and accommodating, and go out of your way to ensure that your guests have a pleasant and enjoyable stay. Pay attention to the little details and anticipate your guests' needs to create a seamless and stress-free experience.

By exceeding your guests' expectations and providing exceptional hospitality, you can create memorable experiences that leave a lasting impression and earn rave reviews and repeat business.

Responding to Guest Feedback

Finally, responding to guest feedback is essential for providing exceptional hospitality and continuously improving the guest experience. Whether positive or negative, guest feedback provides valuable insights into areas where you can excel and areas where you can make improvements.

Here are some tips for responding to guest feedback:

Express gratitude: Start by expressing gratitude to your guests for taking the time to provide feedback, whether positive or negative. Let them know that their feedback is valuable and appreciated and that you're committed to ensuring that they have a positive experience.

Address concerns promptly: If a guest raises a concern or issue in their feedback, address it promptly and professionally. Apologize for any inconvenience or dissatisfaction they may have experienced and take steps to rectify the situation and prevent it from happening again in the future. Be transparent and honest in your response and offer solutions or compensation as appropriate.

Learn from feedback: Use guest feedback as an opportunity to learn and grow as a host. Pay attention to recurring themes or patterns in guest feedback and use this information to identify areas where you can make improvements to enhance the guest experience. Be open to constructive criticism and willing to take action to address areas for improvement.

Take action: Take action on guest feedback by implementing changes or improvements based on their suggestions and recommendations. Let your guests know that their feedback has been heard and that you're committed to making their experience even better in the future. Keep guests informed of any changes or improvements you make based on their feedback to demonstrate your commitment to continuous improvement.

By responding to guest feedback thoughtfully and proactively, you can demonstrate your commitment to providing exceptional hospitality and continuously improving the guest experience.

In this extensive chapter, we've explored the critical importance of understanding guest expectations and providing exceptional hospitality as an Airbnb host. Hospitality is the foundation of the Airbnb experience, and by exceeding your guests' expectations and creating memorable experiences, you can set yourself apart as a superhost and earn rave reviews and repeat business.

By anticipating guest needs, creating a welcoming atmosphere, exceeding guest expectations, and responding to guest feedback, you can ensure that your guests have a positive and enjoyable experience from start to finish. Providing exceptional hospitality is not only about meeting your guests' needs but also about creating lasting connections and fostering a sense of belonging and community.

In the next chapter, we'll delve deeper into the world of Airbnb hosting and explore strategies for optimizing your listing, attracting more guests, and maximizing your earnings.

Chapter 5: Managing Bookings: From Inquiries to Check-Outs

Welcome to Chapter 5 of "From Spare Room to Superhost: Mastering Airbnb's Platform." In this extensive chapter, we will delve into the intricate processes involved in managing bookings on Airbnb, covering everything from handling initial inquiries to facilitating smooth check-outs. As a host, mastering the art of booking management is crucial for providing a seamless and delightful experience for your guests while maximizing your hosting potential. Let's explore the multifaceted aspects of booking management and delve into strategies to ensure efficiency, satisfaction, and success.

Understanding the Booking Process

The booking process on Airbnb is a journey that begins with a guest's initial inquiry and culminates in their check-out from your space. Understanding each stage of this process is vital for effective booking management and ensuring a positive experience for both hosts and guests.

Inquiry Stage: Guests initiate the booking process by sending inquiries to hosts to inquire about availability, rates, and any additional details they may need before proceeding with the booking.

Booking Request: If satisfied with the information provided, guests submit a booking request to the host. The host then has the option to accept, decline, or pre-approve the booking request based on their availability and preferences.

Confirmation: Upon acceptance or pre-approval of the booking request, the booking is confirmed, and the guest's payment is processed, securing their reservation.

Pre-arrival Communication: Leading up to the guest's arrival, hosts and guests may engage in further communication to finalize details such as check-in arrangements, house rules, and any special requests or accommodations.

Check-in and Stay: On the day of arrival, guests check in to the property, and the host welcomes them, providing any necessary information or assistance throughout their stay to ensure a comfortable and enjoyable experience.

Check-out: Upon completion of their stay, guests check out of the property, and the host ensures that the space is clean and ready for the next guest.

By understanding each stage of the booking process, hosts can effectively manage reservations, anticipate guest needs, and provide proactive support throughout the guest's journey.

Handling Inquiries and Booking Requests

Effectively handling inquiries and booking requests is fundamental to attracting guests, securing bookings, and delivering exceptional customer service. Timely and informative communication can make a significant difference in guests' decision-making process and overall satisfaction with their booking experience.

Here are some strategies for handling inquiries and booking requests effectively:

Prompt Response: Respond to inquiries and booking requests promptly, ideally within 24 hours, to demonstrate your responsiveness and commitment to guest satisfaction.

Comprehensive Information: Provide detailed information about your space, including availability, rates, house rules, amenities, and local attractions. Anticipate common questions and proactively address them in your responses to streamline the booking process.

Personalized Communication: Personalize your responses to guests by addressing them by name and referencing specific details from their inquiry or profile. Tailoring your communication shows genuine interest and fosters a connection with potential guests.

Utilize Pre-approval: When appropriate, utilize the pre-approval feature to express your interest in hosting a guest while finalizing booking details. Pre-approval keeps the conversation open and encourages guests to proceed with their reservation.

By implementing these strategies, hosts can effectively engage with potential guests, increase booking conversion rates, and provide a positive booking experience from the outset.

Managing Reservations and Guest Communication

Once a reservation is confirmed, effective reservation management and ongoing guest communication are essential for ensuring a seamless and enjoyable experience for guests throughout their stay. Clear and timely communication helps set expectations, address inquiries or concerns, and build rapport with guests, enhancing their overall satisfaction with the booking process.

Here are some best practices for managing reservations and communicating with guests:

Confirmation Protocol: Confirm reservations promptly upon receipt to reassure guests and solidify their booking. Provide comprehensive information about the reservation, including check-in instructions, house rules, and any additional details pertinent to their stay.

Transparent Expectations: Set clear expectations with guests regarding check-in/out times, house rules, amenities, and any other relevant information. Transparency fosters trust and ensures that guests have a clear understanding of what to expect during their stay.

Proactive Engagement: Be proactive in communicating with guests before and during their stay to address any questions or concerns promptly. Provide contact information and encourage guests to reach out if they need assistance or have inquiries.

Value-Added Information: Offer valuable information and recommendations to enhance guests' stay, such as local attractions, dining options, transportation, and activities. Personalized recommendations demonstrate your commitment to guest satisfaction and enrich the overall guest experience.

By implementing effective reservation management practices and maintaining open lines of communication, hosts can foster positive guest relationships and create memorable experiences that drive guest satisfaction and loyalty.

Facilitating Check-Ins and Check-Outs

The check-in and check-out processes are critical touchpoints in the guest experience, presenting opportunities for hosts to make a lasting impression and ensure a smooth transition for guests into and out of their space. By facilitating these processes with care and efficiency, hosts can elevate the guest experience and leave a positive impression.

Consider the following strategies for facilitating check-ins and check-outs effectively:

Clear Instructions: Provide guests with clear and detailed instructions for check-in, including directions to the property, parking information, and access instructions (e.g., key codes, lockbox codes). Clarity eliminates confusion and minimizes potential issues upon arrival.

Warm Welcome: Welcome guests warmly upon their arrival, whether in person or through digital communication channels. Extend a friendly greeting, offer assistance with luggage, and provide a brief orientation to the space to help guests feel comfortable and at ease.

Comprehensive Walkthrough: Conduct a thorough walkthrough of the property with guests upon check-in to familiarize them with key features, amenities, and operational details. Address any questions or concerns they may have and provide contact information for assistance during their stay.

Efficient Check-Out Process: Streamline the check-out process by providing clear instructions for departure, including any tasks or responsibilities guests are expected to fulfill (e.g., tidying up, returning keys). Express gratitude for their stay and invite feedback to demonstrate your commitment to guest satisfaction.

By prioritizing clear communication, personalized service, and attentive support, hosts can facilitate seamless check-ins and check-outs that contribute to an exceptional guest experience and positive reviews.

Handling Changes and Cancellations

Despite careful planning and preparation, changes or cancellations may occasionally occur, requiring hosts to adapt and navigate these situations with professionalism and flexibility. Handling changes and cancellations effectively is essential for maintaining guest satisfaction, minimizing disruptions, and protecting the integrity of your hosting business.

Consider the following strategies for managing changes and cancellations with grace and efficiency:

Flexibility and Understanding: Demonstrate empathy and understanding when guests request changes or cancellations, recognizing that unforeseen circumstances may necessitate adjustments to their travel plans. Be flexible in accommodating reasonable requests and explore alternative solutions to mitigate any inconvenience.

Transparent Communication: Communicate openly and transparently with guests regarding changes or cancellations, providing timely updates and information as needed. Keep guests informed of any developments and offer assistance in navigating the process to ensure a positive outcome.

Enforce Cancellation Policies: Enforce cancellation policies consistently and fairly in accordance with Airbnb's guidelines and your listing's terms. Clearly communicate your cancellation policy to guests at the time of booking and ensure they understand the associated terms and conditions.

Offer Alternatives: When possible, offer guests alternative options to mitigate the impact of cancellations, such as rescheduling their stay for a later date or providing credits or refunds within the parameters of your cancellation policy. Demonstrating flexibility and willingness to accommodate guests' needs can help preserve guest satisfaction and loyalty.

By approaching changes and cancellations with empathy, transparency, and flexibility, hosts can navigate these situations effectively while upholding the standards of hospitality and professionalism.

In this comprehensive chapter, we've explored the intricacies of managing bookings on Airbnb, from handling initial inquiries to facilitating smooth check-outs. Effective booking management is a cornerstone of successful hosting, encompassing communication, organization, and flexibility to ensure a positive experience for hosts and guests alike.

By mastering the booking process, engaging with guests proactively, facilitating seamless check-ins and check-outs, and navigating changes and cancellations with professionalism and empathy, hosts can elevate the guest experience, drive satisfaction, and cultivate a reputation as a trusted and reliable host.

In the next chapter, we'll delve deeper into the realm of guest experiences, exploring strategies for delighting guests, exceeding expectations, and fostering lasting connections.

Chapter 6: Navigating Communication: Building Rapport with Guests

Welcome to Chapter 6 of "From Spare Room to Superhost: Mastering Airbnb's Platform." In this extensive chapter, we will delve into the intricate art of communication as it pertains to hosting on Airbnb. Effective communication is the cornerstone of successful hosting, facilitating not only the logistical aspects of a guest's stay but also the establishment of trust, the provision of exceptional service, and the cultivation of lasting relationships with guests. Throughout this chapter, we'll explore various strategies and techniques for navigating communication effectively, building rapport with guests, and ensuring a memorable and enjoyable experience for all.

The Importance of Communication in Hospitality

Communication lies at the heart of hospitality, serving as the primary means by which hosts and guests interact, exchange information, and build connections. In the context of Airbnb hosting, effective communication plays a multifaceted role in shaping the guest experience and influencing their overall satisfaction with their stay.

One of the fundamental purposes of communication in hospitality is to establish trust between hosts and guests. Clear, transparent communication helps guests feel confident in their decision to book a property, knowing that their host is accessible, responsive, and committed to ensuring a positive experience. By providing timely and accurate information about the property, addressing any questions or concerns promptly, and communicating openly throughout the guest's stay, hosts can build trust and instill confidence in their guests.

Furthermore, communication is essential for addressing guests' needs and preferences, both before and during their stay. Effective communication allows hosts to gather information about guests' preferences, expectations, and any special requirements they may have, enabling them to tailor the guest experience accordingly. Whether it's providing recommendations for local attractions, accommodating dietary restrictions, or addressing specific requests for amenities or services, clear and proactive communication enables hosts to meet and exceed guest expectations.

Additionally, communication plays a crucial role in resolving any issues or concerns that may arise during a guest's stay. Whether it's a minor maintenance issue, a misunderstanding about house rules, or a request for additional assistance, responsive and effective communication allows hosts to address these challenges promptly and professionally, minimizing any disruptions to the guest experience and preserving guest satisfaction.

Beyond its practical implications, communication also contributes to the overall guest experience by fostering a sense of connection and hospitality. Personalized messages, thoughtful gestures, and genuine interactions help guests feel valued and welcomed, enhancing their emotional connection to the host and the property. By cultivating a warm and hospitable atmosphere through communication, hosts can create memorable experiences that leave a lasting impression on their guests.

In summary, communication is a foundational aspect of hospitality that influences every aspect of the guest experience, from initial inquiries and booking confirmation to check-in, throughout the stay, and beyond. By prioritizing clear, timely, and personalized communication, hosts can create a welcoming and supportive environment that ensures a positive and memorable experience for their guests.

Establishing Communication Channels

A critical aspect of effective communication in Airbnb hosting is the establishment of clear and accessible communication channels through which hosts and guests can connect. Providing multiple channels for communication ensures that guests can reach out to hosts in their preferred method and enables hosts to respond promptly and efficiently to inquiries, requests, and concerns.

Here are some key communication channels that hosts can utilize:

Airbnb Messaging: The Airbnb messaging platform serves as the primary communication channel for hosts and guests to communicate about bookings, inquiries, and other matters related to the reservation. Hosts should monitor their Airbnb inbox regularly and respond to messages promptly to maintain guest satisfaction.

Email: In addition to Airbnb messaging, hosts may choose to communicate with guests via email, particularly for longer or more detailed conversations. Providing guests with a dedicated email address for inquiries or assistance can streamline communication and ensure that important messages are not overlooked.

Phone/Text: Some guests may prefer to communicate via phone or text message, especially for urgent matters or last-minute inquiries. Hosts should provide guests with a contact number where they can reach them directly and be available to respond to calls or texts promptly during their stay.

In-Person Interaction: For hosts who live on-site or nearby, in-person interaction can be a valuable opportunity to connect with guests, address any questions or concerns, and provide personalized recommendations or assistance. Hosts should make themselves available for face-to-face interactions as needed and ensure that guests feel welcome and supported throughout their stay.

By offering multiple communication channels and being responsive to guest inquiries and requests, hosts can create a positive and accessible communication environment that enhances the guest experience.

Pre-Arrival Communication

Effective communication begins before guests arrive, with hosts providing essential information and setting expectations to ensure a smooth and stress-free check-in process. Pre-arrival communication serves as an opportunity for hosts to introduce themselves, provide relevant details about the property and the surrounding area, and address any questions or concerns that guests may have.

Here are some key elements of pre-arrival communication:

Check-In Instructions: Provide detailed check-in instructions to guests, including directions to the property, parking information, and access instructions (e.g., key codes, lockbox codes). Clear and comprehensive instructions minimize confusion and ensure that guests can easily access the property upon arrival.

House Rules and Guidelines: Clearly communicate the house rules and guidelines to guests before their arrival, outlining expectations regarding noise levels, smoking, pets, and any other relevant policies. Reinforce the importance of adhering to the rules to maintain a harmonious environment for all guests.

Amenities and Facilities: Highlight the amenities and facilities available to guests during their stay, such as Wi-Fi access, laundry facilities, and recreational areas. Provide instructions for accessing and using these amenities to ensure that guests can fully enjoy their stay.

Local Recommendations: Offer recommendations for local attractions, restaurants, shops, and activities to help guests make the most of their time in the area. Provide insider tips and personalized recommendations based on the guest's interests and preferences to enhance their overall experience.

By communicating proactively with guests before their arrival, hosts can anticipate their needs, address any questions or concerns, and create a positive first impression that sets the stage for a memorable stay.

Ongoing Communication During the Stay

Effective communication doesn't end once guests have checked in; it's an ongoing process that continues throughout their stay. Hosts should remain accessible and responsive to guest inquiries and requests, providing assistance and support as needed to ensure a comfortable and enjoyable experience.

Here are some strategies for ongoing communication during the guest's stay:

Welcome Message: Send a welcome message to guests shortly after their arrival to greet them, confirm that they've settled in comfortably, and help with any questions or concerns they may have. A warm and personalized welcome message helps guests feel valued and sets a positive tone for their stay.

Check-In Messages: Check in with guests periodically during their stay to ensure that everything is going smoothly and address any questions or issues that may arise. Offer assistance with restaurant reservations, transportation arrangements, or other requests to enhance the guest experience.

Respond Promptly: Respond to guest messages and inquiries promptly, ideally within a few hours or less. Guests appreciate timely responses and may become frustrated or concerned if they don't receive a response promptly.

Be Available: Make yourself available to guests for assistance and support throughout their stay. Provide contact information and encourage guests to reach out if they have any questions or concerns, assuring them that you're available to help.

By maintaining open lines of communication and being attentive to guest needs, hosts can foster positive guest experiences and build rapport that leads to repeat bookings and referrals.

Post-Stay Communication

After guests have checked out, hosts should follow up with a post-stay message to express gratitude for their visit, solicit feedback, and encourage future bookings. Post-stay communication provides an opportunity to leave a lasting impression on guests and gather valuable insights to improve the guest experience.

Here are some elements to include in post-stay communication:

Thank-You Message: Send a thank-you message to guests after their departure to express gratitude for choosing to stay with you. Thank them for their visit and acknowledge any positive feedback or contributions they made during their stay.

Request Feedback: Encourage guests to share their feedback and experiences from their stay, both positive and constructive. Ask specific questions about their experience, such as what they enjoyed most about their stay and any areas for improvement.

Provide Contact Information: Provide guests with your contact information and invite them to reach out if they have any questions or concerns or if they would like to book a future stay. Reinforce your commitment to providing excellent customer service and maintaining open lines of communication.

Offer Incentives: Consider offering incentives or discounts for future bookings as a token of appreciation for guests' loyalty and feedback. Providing incentives encourages repeat bookings and fosters a sense of goodwill and appreciation.

By following up with guests after their stay and soliciting feedback, hosts can demonstrate their commitment to guest satisfaction, gather valuable insights, and build lasting relationships that lead to continued success as a host.

Handling Communication Challenges

While effective communication is essential for successful hosting, hosts may encounter challenges or obstacles that require careful navigation. From language barriers to misunderstandings, handling communication challenges with grace and professionalism is crucial for maintaining positive guest relationships and preserving the integrity of the hosting experience.

Here are some strategies for addressing common communication challenges:

Language Barriers: If language barriers exist between hosts and guests, consider using translation tools or enlisting the help of a multilingual staff member or friend to facilitate communication. Keep messages clear and concise and use simple language to ensure understanding.

Misunderstandings: If misunderstandings occur, address them promptly and transparently to clarify any confusion and prevent further escalation. Apologize for any confusion or inconvenience and take steps to rectify the situation to the best of your ability.

Difficult Guests: In some cases, hosts may encounter difficult or demanding guests who present communication challenges. Remain calm and professional and strive to address their concerns and requests in a timely and respectful manner. Set clear boundaries and enforce house rules as needed to maintain a harmonious environment for all guests.

Technical Issues: Technical issues such as Wi-Fi outages or property maintenance problems may impact communication with guests. Keep guests informed of any technical issues or disruptions and provide updates on efforts to resolve the problem promptly. Offer alternative solutions or accommodations as needed to minimize inconvenience.

By approaching communication challenges with patience, empathy, and professionalism, hosts can navigate difficult situations effectively and preserve positive guest relationships.

In this comprehensive chapter, we've explored the critical role of communication in building rapport with guests and enhancing the overall guest experience. Effective communication is essential for establishing trust, addressing guest needs, and fostering positive relationships that lead to repeat bookings and referrals.

By prioritizing clear and transparent communication, providing multiple channels for interaction, and engaging with guests proactively throughout their stay, hosts can create a welcoming and supportive environment that ensures a positive and memorable experience for their guests.

In the next chapter, we'll delve into strategies for managing guest expectations and delivering exceptional hospitality that sets hosts apart as superhosts.

31

Chapter 7: Handling Challenges: Dealing with Difficult Guests and Situations

Welcome to Chapter 7 of "From Spare Room to Superhost: Mastering Airbnb's Platform." In this comprehensive chapter, we'll delve into the multifaceted world of handling challenges that hosts may encounter while managing their Airbnb listings and interacting with guests. While the majority of guests are respectful and easy to accommodate, there are instances when hosts may encounter difficult guests or face unexpected situations that require skillful navigation and effective problem-solving strategies. By equipping themselves with a robust toolkit for handling these challenges, hosts can maintain professionalism, preserve the integrity of their hosting business, and ensure that the guest experience remains positive and memorable.

Understanding Difficult Guests and Situations

Difficult guests and challenging situations can manifest in various forms, each presenting its own set of unique challenges for hosts. Recognizing the signs of difficult guests and situations is the first step towards effectively managing these scenarios.

Demanding Guests: These guests may have high expectations or specific preferences regarding their stay, such as requesting additional amenities or accommodations beyond what is typically offered in the listing.

Disruptive Guests: Disruptive guests may engage in behavior that disturbs other guests or violates house rules, such as excessive noise, parties, or unauthorized guests.

Complaining Guests: These guests may voice complaints or grievances about various aspects of their stay, ranging from cleanliness issues to communication challenges.

Non-Compliant Guests: Non-compliant guests may disregard house rules or policies, such as smoking in non-smoking areas, bringing pets without permission, or violating occupancy limits.

Emergency Situations: Hosts may also encounter unexpected emergencies or unforeseen circumstances, such as property damage, accidents, or natural disasters, which require prompt action and effective crisis management.

By understanding the different types of difficult guests and situations, hosts can better prepare themselves to handle these challenges proactively and mitigate their impact on the guest experience and their hosting business.

Strategies for Dealing with Difficult Guests

When faced with difficult guests, hosts can employ a variety of strategies to manage the situation effectively while maintaining professionalism and guest satisfaction. Here are some tips for handling difficult guests:

Remain Calm: It's essential to stay calm and composed when interacting with difficult guests, even in challenging situations. Responding with a calm and collected demeanor can help de-escalate tensions and facilitate more productive communication.

Listen Actively: Actively listen to the guest's concerns or grievances and demonstrate empathy and understanding. Let them know that their concerns are being heard and taken seriously, even if you may not agree with their perspective.

Communicate Clearly: Clearly communicate your expectations and boundaries to the guest in a firm but respectful manner. Reinforce any house rules or policies that have been violated and explain the consequences of non-compliance.

Offer Solutions: Work with the guest to find practical solutions or alternatives to address their concerns and resolve the issue satisfactorily. Be flexible and accommodating within reason, but also assertive in upholding the integrity of your hosting business.

Document Incidents: Keep detailed records of any incidents or interactions with difficult guests, including timestamps, relevant details, and communication exchanges. This documentation may be useful for resolving disputes or providing evidence if necessary.

Seek Support: If the situation escalates or becomes unmanageable, don't hesitate to seek support or assistance from Airbnb's support team or local authorities. They can provide guidance and assistance in resolving disputes and enforcing policies.

Responding to Complaints and Feedback

In addition to dealing with difficult guests in real-time, hosts must also be prepared to respond to complaints and feedback from guests after their stay. Here's how to handle complaints and feedback effectively:

Acknowledge the Issue: Acknowledge the guest's concerns or grievances and apologize for any inconvenience or dissatisfaction they may have experienced during their stay. Express empathy and understanding to validate the guest's feelings.

Offer Solutions: Provide practical solutions or remedies to address the guest's concerns and resolve the issue satisfactorily. Offer a partial refund, a discount on a future stay, or implement changes to prevent similar issues from occurring in the future.

Take Action: Take proactive steps to address any underlying issues or shortcomings identified in the guest's feedback. This may involve improving cleanliness standards, upgrading amenities, or enhancing communication processes.

Follow Up: Follow up with the guest after addressing their concerns to ensure that they are satisfied with the resolution and to thank them for bringing the issue to your attention. This demonstrates your commitment to guest satisfaction and helps rebuild trust with the guest.

Learn and Improve: Use feedback from guests as an opportunity for learning and improvement. Identify areas where your hosting practices can be strengthened and implement changes accordingly.

Preventing and Managing Conflict

Preventing conflicts before they arise is preferable to resolving them after they occur. Hosts can take proactive steps to prevent conflicts and minimize the likelihood of difficult guest interactions by:

Setting Clear Expectations: Establish clear expectations for guests by outlining house rules, policies, and guidelines in your listing description and communication with guests.

Providing Detailed Information: Provide guests with detailed information about the property, amenities, and local area to set realistic expectations and help them make informed decisions about their stay.

Communicating Proactively: Communicate proactively with guests before, during, and after their stay to address any questions or concerns they may have and ensure a smooth and enjoyable experience.

Establishing Boundaries: Set clear boundaries with guests regarding acceptable behavior, noise levels, and respect for the property and other guests. Enforce house rules consistently and fairly to maintain a safe and comfortable environment for all guests.

Resolving Issues Promptly: Address any issues or concerns that arise during a guest's stay promptly and professionally to prevent escalation and minimize disruptions to the guest experience.

Seeking Mediation: In cases where conflicts arise that cannot be resolved independently, consider seeking mediation or assistance from Airbnb's support team to facilitate communication and reach a resolution that satisfies all parties.

In this extensive chapter, we've explored the myriad of challenges that hosts may encounter while managing their Airbnb listings and interacting with guests. From dealing with difficult guests to addressing complaints and conflicts, handling these challenges requires skill, patience, and effective communication.

By equipping themselves with strategies for handling difficult guests and situations, hosts can navigate these challenges confidently and professionally, ensuring that the guest experience remains positive and memorable. By prioritizing guest satisfaction, maintaining open lines of communication, and taking proactive steps to prevent and resolve conflicts, hosts can create a welcoming and supportive environment that ensures a memorable and enjoyable experience for their guests.

In the next chapter, we'll explore strategies for creating an unforgettable guest experience and delivering exceptional hospitality that sets hosts apart as superhosts.

Chapter 8: Enhancing Your Space: Tips for Design and Amenities

Welcome to Chapter 8 of "From Spare Room to Superhost: Mastering Airbnb's Platform." In this comprehensive chapter, we'll delve deep into the art of enhancing your space to create an unforgettable experience for your guests. From the layout and design to the amenities you offer, every aspect of your space contributes to the overall guest experience and can set you apart as a top-rated host. Whether you're a new host looking to create a welcoming environment or an experienced host seeking to elevate your listing to superhost status, this chapter will provide you with practical tips and strategies to enhance your space and delight your guests.

The Importance of Space Enhancement

Enhancing your space goes beyond mere aesthetics; it's about creating an immersive experience that leaves a lasting impression on your guests. Here's why space enhancement is crucial:

Guest Comfort: The primary goal of space enhancement is to ensure guest comfort. A well-designed and well-appointed space makes guests feel at home and enhances their overall satisfaction with their stay.

Positive First Impressions: The initial impression guests have of your space sets the tone for their entire stay. By investing in high-quality furnishings, stylish decor, and thoughtful amenities, you can create a positive first impression that sets you apart from the competition.

Differentiation: With thousands of listings on Airbnb, it's essential to differentiate your space. Unique design elements, personalized touches, and standout amenities can help your listing stand out and attract more bookings.

Guest Satisfaction: Satisfied guests are more likely to leave positive reviews, recommend your listing to others, and return for future stays. By prioritizing space enhancement, you can enhance guest satisfaction and cultivate a loyal base of repeat guests.

Higher Ratings and Earnings: Listings that offer exceptional design and amenities tend to receive higher ratings and command higher nightly rates. By investing in your space, you can increase your earning potential and achieve superhost status.

In summary, space enhancement is a critical aspect of successful hosting that can significantly impact guest satisfaction, ratings, and earnings. By paying attention to the details and creating a welcoming and memorable environment, you can delight your guests and ensure they have an unforgettable stay.

Designing Your Space

The design of your space plays a significant role in shaping the guest experience and influencing their perception of your listing. Whether you're starting from scratch or updating an existing space, here are some key principles to keep in mind:

Define Your Style: Start by defining the overall style and aesthetic you want to achieve for your space. Consider factors such as the property's location, architecture, and target audience when choosing a design theme. Whether it's modern and minimalist, cozy and rustic, or chic and urban, ensure that the design reflects your personality and resonates with your guests.

Prioritize Comfort: Comfort should be a top priority when designing your space. Choose comfortable furnishings, such as sofas, chairs, and beds, with high-quality materials and supportive features. Invest in soft bedding, fluffy pillows, and cozy throws to create a warm and inviting atmosphere.

Maximize Functionality: A well-designed space maximizes functionality and efficiency, allowing guests to make the most of their stay. Arrange furniture to optimize traffic flow and usability, and to ensure essential amenities are easily accessible. Consider multifunctional furniture pieces that serve multiple purposes to maximize space in smaller accommodations.

Create Focal Points: Incorporate focal points into your design to draw attention and create visual interest. This could be a statement piece of furniture, a striking piece of artwork, or a feature wall with bold colors or patterns. Focal points help to anchor the space and add personality and character to your listing.

Pay Attention to Lighting: Lighting plays a crucial role in setting the mood and ambiance of your space. Incorporate a mix of ambient, task, and accent lighting to create layers of illumination that can be adjusted to suit different activities and occasions. Consider natural light sources, such as windows and skylights, to enhance brightness and create a sense of spaciousness.

Add Personal Touches: Personalize your space with unique touches and accessories that reflect your personality and make guests feel welcome. Display local artwork, souvenirs, or photographs that showcase the character and charm of the area. Provide thoughtful amenities, such as books, board games, or travel guides, that add value and enhance the guest experience.

By following these design principles and incorporating thoughtful touches into your space, you can create a visually stunning and comfortable environment that delights your guests and leaves a lasting impression.

Selecting Amenities

Amenities play a significant role in enhancing the guest-experience and providing added value during their stay. From essential conveniences to luxury indulgences, the amenities you offer can significantly impact guest satisfaction and influence their decision to book your listing. Here are some key considerations when selecting amenities for your space:

Essential Amenities: Start by providing essential amenities that guests expect to find in comfortable and well-equipped accommodation. This includes basic necessities such as clean linens, towels, toiletries, and kitchen essentials like cookware, dishes, and utensils. Ensure that these amenities are in good condition and readily available to guests upon their arrival.

Comfort Enhancers: Consider amenities that enhance comfort and convenience for your guests, such as high-quality bedding and pillows, blackout curtains or blinds for restful sleep, and climate control systems to maintain optimal temperature levels. Other comfort-enhancing amenities may include fans, heaters, or air purifiers to accommodate guests' individual preferences and needs.

Technology and Entertainment: In today's digital age, guests expect access to technology and entertainment amenities to stay connected and entertained during their stay. Provide amenities such as high-speed Wi-Fi, smart TVs with streaming services, Bluetooth speakers, and charging stations for electronic devices. Consider offering access to streaming platforms or subscription services for added convenience and entertainment options.

Kitchen and Dining Supplies: If your listing includes a kitchen or kitchenette, ensure that it is well-stocked with essential supplies and appliances for cooking and dining. Provide cooking basics like oil, salt, and spices, as well as cookware, utensils, and appliances such as a stove, oven, microwave, toaster, and coffee maker. Consider offering complimentary coffee, tea, and snacks for an extra touch of hospitality.

Bathroom Amenities: Pay attention to the amenities provided in the bathroom to enhance guest comfort and convenience. Offer high-quality toiletries such as shampoo, conditioner, body wash, and hand soap, as well as plush towels and bathrobes for added luxury. Consider installing features like a rainfall showerhead or a bathtub for a spa-like experience.

Safety and Security: Ensure that your space is equipped with safety and security amenities to provide peace of mind for your guests. This may include smoke detectors, carbon monoxide alarms, fire extinguishers, and first aid kits for emergencies. Provide clear instructions on how to use these amenities and where to find them in case of an emergency.

Outdoor and Recreational Amenities: If your property has outdoor space or recreational facilities, consider providing amenities that enhance the outdoor experience for your guests. This could include outdoor furniture, barbecue grills, fire pits, bicycles, kayaks, or beach equipment, depending on your location and property type. Offer guests access to amenities such as swimming pools, hot tubs, or fitness facilities if available.

Sustainable and Eco-Friendly Amenities: Increasingly, guests are seeking eco-friendly accommodations that prioritize sustainability and environmental responsibility. Consider offering amenities such as energy-efficient appliances, LED lighting, recycling bins, and reusable water bottles to minimize environmental impact and appeal to eco-conscious travelers.

When selecting amenities for your space, consider the preferences and needs of your target audience, as well as the unique features and characteristics of your property. By providing a thoughtful selection of amenities that enhance comfort, convenience, and enjoyment, you can create a memorable and rewarding experience for your guests.

Implementing Design and Amenity Upgrades

Once you've identified the design elements and amenities you want to incorporate into your space, it's time to put your plan into action. Implementing design and amenity upgrades requires careful planning, budgeting, and execution to ensure a successful outcome. Here are some steps to consider when implementing upgrades:

Assess Your Space: Start by assessing your space to identify areas for improvement and determine which design elements and amenities will have the most significant impact on the guest experience. Consider factors such as the layout, size, and functionality of the space, as well as any existing features or furnishings that can be retained or repurposed.

Set a Budget: Establish a budget for your design and amenity upgrades based on your financial resources and priorities. Allocate funds for essential upgrades first, such as replacing worn-out furnishings or upgrading essential amenities, before allocating funds for discretionary upgrades or enhancements.

Prioritize Upgrades: Prioritize upgrades based on their potential impact on the guest experience and your overall hosting goals. Focus on upgrades that enhance comfort, convenience, and aesthetics while aligning with your target audience's preferences and needs.

Research Suppliers and Vendors: Research suppliers and vendors to source materials, furnishings, and amenities for your upgrades. Compare prices, quality, and reviews to ensure you're getting the best value for your investment. Consider partnering with local artisans or suppliers to support small businesses and add a unique touch to your space.

Plan Your Timeline: Create a timeline for implementing your upgrades, considering factors such as lead times for ordering materials, scheduling contractors or service providers, and coordinating with existing bookings or guest stays. Allow ample time for each phase of the upgrade process to ensure a smooth and timely completion.

Coordinate Logistics: Coordinate logistics for your upgrades, including scheduling deliveries, coordinating installations, and arranging for disposal of old materials or furnishings. Communicate with contractors, vendors, and service providers to ensure everyone is on the same page and working towards a common goal.

Monitor Progress: Monitor the progress of your upgrades closely to ensure that work is progressing according to plan and within budget. Address any issues or challenges that arise promptly and communicate with your team to find solutions and keep the project on track.

Inspect and Test: Once the upgrades are complete, inspect the finished work to ensure that everything meets your expectations and quality standards. Test amenities and appliances to ensure they are functioning correctly and address any issues or deficiencies promptly.

Solicit Feedback: Solicit feedback from guests after they've experienced the upgrades to gauge their satisfaction and identify any areas for improvement. Use guest feedback to fine-tune your offerings and make adjustments as needed to enhance the guest experience further.

By following these steps and taking a strategic approach to implementing design and amenity upgrades, you can enhance your space and create a more inviting and memorable experience for your guests.

In this extensive chapter, we've explored the importance of enhancing your space to create a welcoming and memorable experience for your guests. From thoughtful design elements to thoughtful amenities, every detail of your space contributes to the overall guest experience and can set you apart as a superhost.

By prioritizing space enhancement, investing in high-quality furnishings and amenities, and incorporating thoughtful touches into your space, you can elevate the guest experience and attract more bookings. By creating a comfortable, stylish, and well-equipped environment, you can delight your guests and ensure that they have a memorable and enjoyable stay.

In the next chapter, we'll delve into strategies for marketing and promoting your Airbnb listing to attract more guests and maximize your earning potential.

Chapter 9: Becoming a Superhost: Requirements and Benefits

Welcome to Chapter 9 of "From Spare Room to Superhost: Mastering Airbnb's Platform." In this comprehensive chapter, we'll explore the prestigious status of being a Superhost on Airbnb, delve into the specific requirements needed to achieve this title, highlight the various benefits it offers hosts, and provide detailed strategies for successfully attaining and maintaining Superhost status. Whether you're a new host aiming to reach this milestone or an experienced host seeking to elevate your hosting game, this chapter will equip you with the knowledge and tools to excel on the platform.

Understanding the Superhost Status

The Superhost status is Airbnb's highest recognition for hosts who consistently provide exceptional hospitality and create memorable experiences for their guests. This prestigious title is awarded to hosts who meet specific criteria demonstrating their commitment to superior service, including:

Host Activity: Superhosts must demonstrate a high level of activity on the platform by hosting a certain number of stays within the past year. This requirement ensures that Superhosts are actively engaged in hosting and regularly welcoming guests into their accommodations.

Response Rate: Superhosts are expected to maintain a high response rate to guest inquiries and booking requests, typically above 90%. Prompt and effective communication is essential for providing excellent customer service and ensuring guest satisfaction.

Acceptance Rate: Superhosts should also maintain a high acceptance rate for booking requests, typically above 90%. Accepting a high percentage of booking requests demonstrates reliability and availability to guests, enhancing their booking experience.

Overall Rating: Superhosts must maintain a minimum overall rating, typically 4.8 stars or higher, based on guest reviews. High ratings reflect guest satisfaction with the host's hospitality, accommodations, and overall experience.

Commitment to Airbnb's Community Standards: Superhosts are expected to uphold Airbnb's community standards and adhere to its policies and guidelines. This includes providing accurate listing descriptions, respecting guest privacy, and resolving any issues or disputes promptly and professionally.

By meeting these criteria, hosts can qualify for Superhost status and enjoy the numerous benefits it offers, including increased visibility, credibility, and earning potential.

Benefits of Being a Superhost

Achieving Superhost status comes with a range of benefits that can significantly enhance a host's experience on Airbnb. Let's explore some of the key benefits of being a Superhost:

Increased Visibility: Superhosts receive enhanced visibility in Airbnb's search results and are featured more prominently on the platform. This increased exposure can attract more views and bookings for your listing, helping you reach a broader audience of potential guests.

Credibility and Trust: Superhost status serves as a badge of credibility and trust, signaling to guests that you are a reliable and experienced host who consistently delivers exceptional hospitality. Guests are more likely to book with Superhosts, knowing they can expect a high standard of service and accommodations.

Higher Search Rankings: Superhosts often receive preferential treatment in Airbnb's search algorithm, appearing higher in search results compared to non-Superhost listings. This improved visibility can lead to more bookings and greater success as a host.

Improved Booking Conversion: Guests are more likely to book with Superhosts due to their reputation for excellence in hospitality and positive guest reviews. This can result in higher booking conversion rates and increased occupancy for your listing.

Premium Support: Superhosts have access to premium support from Airbnb's customer service team, including dedicated assistance with inquiries, issues, and emergencies. This priority support ensures that Superhosts receive prompt and personalized assistance to resolve any concerns and provide a seamless guest experience.

Exclusive Discounts and Offers: Airbnb occasionally offers exclusive discounts, promotions, and perks to Superhosts as a reward for their outstanding performance and loyalty to the platform. These benefits may include discounted booking fees, credits towards future stays, or access to special events and experiences.

Superhost Badge: Superhosts receive a prestigious Superhost badge on their Airbnb profile, showcasing their status to guests and fellow hosts. The Superhost badge serves as a mark of excellence and distinguishes Superhosts from other hosts on the platform.

Professional Development Opportunities: Airbnb provides Superhosts with access to educational resources, training programs, and networking opportunities to support their professional development and growth as hosts. These resources can help Superhosts enhance their hosting skills, optimize their listings, and stay informed about industry trends and best practices.

Overall, being a Superhost offers numerous benefits that can elevate a host's experience and contribute to their success on Airbnb. By meeting the requirements and maintaining Superhost status, hosts can enjoy increased visibility, credibility, and earning potential while providing exceptional hospitality to their guests.

Strategies for Achieving Superhost Status

Becoming a Superhost requires dedication, commitment, and attention to detail. Here are some strategies to help hosts achieve Superhost status:

Provide Outstanding Hospitality: Focus on providing exceptional hospitality to guests by offering personalized service, anticipating their needs, and exceeding their expectations. Create a welcoming and comfortable environment and go the extra mile to ensure that guests have a memorable experience.

Maintain High Standards: Uphold high standards for cleanliness, maintenance, and guest communication throughout the entire guest experience. Respond promptly to inquiries and booking requests, address any issues or concerns promptly, and strive to deliver consistent quality across all aspects of the listing.

Solicit Positive Reviews: Encourage guests to leave positive reviews by providing excellent service and accommodations during their stay. Communicate with guests throughout their stay to ensure their needs are met and follow up after their departure to thank them for their feedback and encourage them to leave a review.

Optimize Your Listing: Optimize the listing to attract more guests and improve search rankings. Use high-quality photos and detailed descriptions to showcase the space, highlight unique features and amenities, and set realistic expectations for guests.

Stay Active and Engaged: Stay active and engaged on the platform by regularly updating the calendar, responding to guest inquiries and messages promptly, and participating in Airbnb's community forums and events. Demonstrate a commitment to hosting by maintaining a consistent presence on the platform.

Seek Feedback and Continuous Improvement: Solicit feedback from guests to identify areas for improvement and implement changes to enhance the guest experience. Regularly review guest feedback and ratings to identify trends and patterns and take proactive steps to address any issues or concerns raised by guests.

Stay Informed About Airbnb's Policies: Stay informed about Airbnb's policies, guidelines, and best practices for hosting to ensure compliance and avoid potential violations. Familiarize yourself with Airbnb's community standards, cancellation policies, and hosting requirements to provide a seamless and compliant guest experience.

By following these strategies and focusing on providing exceptional hospitality, hosts can increase their chances of achieving Superhost status and enjoy the benefits it offers.

Maintaining Superhost Status

Once Superhost status is achieved, it's essential to maintain it by continuing to deliver exceptional hospitality and meeting Airbnb's requirements. Here are some tips for maintaining Superhost status:

Consistency is Key: Maintain consistency in hosting practices and uphold the high standards that earned Superhost status. Provide the same level of service and accommodations to every guest, regardless of their length of stay or booking preferences.

Stay Active and Responsive: Continue to stay active and responsive on the platform by promptly responding to guest inquiries and messages, updating the calendar regularly, and keeping listing information accurate and up to date. Be proactive in addressing guest concerns and resolving any issues that arise during their stay.

Monitor Ratings and Reviews: Monitor ratings and reviews closely to identify trends or patterns indicating areas for improvement. Pay attention to guest feedback and take constructive criticism into account when making changes to the listing or hosting practices.

Strive for Excellence: Continue to strive for excellence in every aspect of the hosting experience, from cleanliness and communication to guest satisfaction and overall hospitality. Look for opportunities to enhance the guest experience and exceed expectations whenever possible.

Seek Support and Resources: Take advantage of Airbnb's support resources and educational materials to stay informed about best practices for hosting and to address any questions or concerns. Participate in host education programs, webinars, and community forums to connect with other hosts and share insights and experiences.

Adapt to Changes: Stay adaptable and flexible in response to changes in the travel industry, guest preferences, and Airbnb's policies and guidelines. Be proactive in implementing any updates or changes to the listing or hosting practices to ensure compliance and maintain a positive guest experience.

By staying committed to excellence, remaining active and engaged on the platform, and continuously seeking feedback and improvement, hosts can maintain Superhost status and continue to enjoy the benefits it offers.

In this comprehensive chapter, we've explored the prestigious status of being a Superhost on Airbnb, the requirements needed to achieve this title, the benefits it offers hosts, and strategies for success. Becoming a Superhost is a significant milestone for hosts, signifying excellence in hospitality and superior guest satisfaction.

By understanding the requirements for Superhost status, implementing strategies to achieve it, and maintaining high standards of hospitality, hosts can elevate their hosting experience and attract more guests to their listings.

Superhost status offers numerous benefits, including increased visibility, credibility, and earning potential, making it a valuable achievement for any host on Airbnb.

In the next chapter, we'll delve into advanced hosting strategies and tips for maximizing success as a Superhost. Whether hosts are striving to achieve Superhost status or looking to maintain their status, these strategies will help them take their hosting to the next level.

Chapter 10: Growing Your Business: Scaling Up and Expanding Your Hosting Reach

Welcome to Chapter 10 of "From Spare Room to Superhost: Mastering Airbnb's Platform." In this extensive chapter, we'll delve into the multifaceted process of growing your Airbnb business, covering everything from scaling up your operations to expanding your hosting reach. Whether you're a novice host seeking to broaden your portfolio or an established Superhost aiming to increase your earnings and market share, this chapter will equip you with comprehensive insights and actionable strategies to propel your hosting business to new heights.

Assessing Your Growth Potential

Before embarking on a journey to grow your Airbnb business, it's imperative to conduct a thorough assessment of your current situation and potential for expansion. Here's how you can evaluate your growth potential:

Current Performance Analysis: Begin by scrutinizing your current performance metrics, including occupancy rates, average nightly rates, and guest satisfaction scores. This analysis will provide valuable insights into your strengths and areas that require improvement, serving as a foundation for your growth strategy.

Resource Evaluation: Assess the resources at your disposal, encompassing the number of properties in your portfolio, available capital for investment, and your bandwidth to manage additional listings. Understanding your resource constraints will help you devise a realistic growth plan aligned with your capabilities.

Market Research: Dive into market research to gauge the demand for short-term rentals in your area and identify potential opportunities for expansion. Analyze factors such as tourism trends, local events, and competitor offerings to pinpoint lucrative niches and untapped markets.

Target Audience Identification: Define your target audience and gain deep insights into their preferences, needs, and booking behaviors. Tailor your growth strategy to resonate with your target demographic, ensuring that your offerings cater to their specific requirements.

By conducting a comprehensive assessment of your growth potential, you'll be better equipped to formulate a strategic roadmap for scaling up your Airbnb business.

Strategies for Scaling Up Your Airbnb Business

Scaling up your Airbnb business requires a well-executed strategy encompassing various facets of operations and marketing. Here are some proven strategies to consider:

Expand Your Portfolio: Explore opportunities to diversify and expand your portfolio by acquiring additional properties or collaborating with other property owners. Focus on properties that complement your existing listings and cater to the preferences of your target audience.

Diversify Your Offerings: Broaden your offerings to appeal to a wider range of guests and capture diverse market segments. Consider offering different types of accommodations, such as entire homes, private rooms, or unique stays, to accommodate varying traveler preferences and budgets.

Optimize Pricing and Revenue Management: Implement dynamic pricing strategies and revenue management techniques to maximize your earnings and occupancy rates. Leverage data analytics and pricing algorithms to adjust your rates dynamically based on demand, seasonality, and competitor pricing.

Streamline Operations: Invest in automation and technology to streamline your operations and enhance efficiency. Utilize property management software, channel managers, and automated messaging systems to manage reservations, coordinate cleaning and maintenance, and communicate with guests seamlessly.

Enhance Guest Experience: Prioritize guest experience by providing exceptional service and amenities that exceed expectations. Invest in quality furnishings, amenities, and thoughtful touches to create memorable stays and foster positive guest reviews and recommendations.

Implement Marketing and Branding Strategies: Develop a strong brand identity and marketing strategy to differentiate your listings and attract more guests. Utilize a mix of online and offline channels, including social media, email marketing, and partnerships, to promote your properties and engage with potential guests.

Expand to New Markets: Explore opportunities to expand your hosting reach by targeting new markets and demographics. Consider listing your properties on additional booking platforms, partnering with local businesses, or offering specialized packages to attract guests from different regions or segments.

Invest in Professional Development: Continuously invest in your professional development as a host by attending industry conferences, workshops, and training programs. Stay abreast of industry trends, best practices, and regulatory changes to enhance your hosting skills and stay ahead of the curve.

By implementing these strategies systematically and thoughtfully, you can scale up your Airbnb business and unlock new growth opportunities in the competitive vacation rental market.

Leveraging Technology and Tools for Growth

Technology and tools play a pivotal role in facilitating the growth and expansion of your Airbnb business. Here are some essential technologies and tools to leverage:

Property Management Software: Invest in robust property management software to centralize reservation management, automate tasks, and streamline operations. Look for features such as calendar synchronization, guest communication tools, and performance analytics to optimize efficiency.

Dynamic Pricing Tools: Harness the power of dynamic pricing tools to adjust your rates dynamically based on market demand, competitor pricing, and booking trends. Utilize data-driven insights and algorithms to optimize your pricing strategy and maximize revenue potential.

Channel Managers: Utilize channel managers to synchronize your listings across multiple booking platforms and reach a broader audience of travelers. Streamline the distribution process, prevent double bookings, and maintain consistency across all platforms with a reliable channel management solution.

Guest Communication Platforms: Adopt guest communication platforms that enable seamless communication with guests throughout their journey. Leverage automated messaging, multilingual support, and guest feedback management tools to enhance the guest experience and foster positive interactions.

Smart Home Technology: Incorporate smart home technology into your properties to enhance convenience, security, and sustainability. Install smart locks, thermostats, lighting, and security cameras to improve guest comfort and streamline property management tasks.

Data Analytics Tools: Utilize data analytics tools to gain actionable insights into your performance, track key metrics, and make data-driven decisions. Analyze booking patterns, guest demographics, and revenue trends to identify opportunities for optimization and growth.

By leveraging technology and tools effectively, you can streamline operations, enhance guest satisfaction, and drive sustainable growth for your Airbnb business.

Forming Strategic Partnerships for Expansion

Strategic partnerships can be instrumental in expanding your hosting reach and tapping into new markets. Here are some strategic partnerships to consider:

Local Businesses and Attractions: Collaborate with local businesses, attractions, and tour operators to offer exclusive experiences and packages to your guests. Partner with restaurants, spas, and recreational facilities to provide added value and enhance the guest experience.

Tourism Organizations: Forge partnerships with tourism organizations, convention bureaus, and destination marketing agencies to promote your properties to travelers visiting your area. Participate in tourism campaigns, events, and promotional activities to increase visibility and attract more guests.

Corporate Housing Providers: Partner with corporate housing providers, relocation companies, and business travel agencies to cater to the needs of business travelers and professionals. Offer corporate rates, long-term stays, and business-friendly amenities to attract this lucrative market segment.

Event Planners and Wedding Coordinators: Collaborate with event planners, wedding coordinators, and special event venues to accommodate guests attending weddings, conferences, and other events. Offer group discounts, event packages, and customized services to meet their specific needs.

Online Travel Agencies (OTAs): Expand your reach by listing your properties on additional online travel agencies and vacation rental platforms besides Airbnb. Platforms such as Booking.com, Vrbo, and Expedia can help you reach a broader audience of travelers and increase your booking potential.

By forming strategic partnerships with these entities, you can extend your reach, access new customer segments, and generate incremental bookings for your properties.

Investing in Growth and Expansion Initiatives

Investing in growth and expansion initiatives is essential for fueling the long-term success and sustainability of your Airbnb business. Here are some key areas to invest in:

Property Acquisition and Renovation: Allocate funds for acquiring additional properties or renovating existing ones to expand your portfolio and enhance the guest experience. Focus on properties in high-demand locations with potential for growth and improvement.

Marketing and Advertising: Invest in marketing and advertising campaigns to promote your properties and attract more guests. Utilize targeted advertising on social media, search engines, and travel websites to reach your target audience effectively and drive bookings.

Professional Services: Consider outsourcing certain tasks and hiring professional services to streamline your operations and ensure the highest standards of service and cleanliness. Invest in property management companies, cleaning services, and maintenance contractors to manage your properties efficiently.

Technology and Automation: Invest in technology and automation tools to optimize your operations, enhance guest satisfaction, and drive growth. Consider investing in property management software, dynamic pricing tools, and smart home technology to improve efficiency and effectiveness.

Training and Development: Allocate resources for training and development programs for yourself and your team to enhance your hosting skills and stay competitive. Attend workshops, seminars, and conferences to learn from industry experts and network with other hosts.

By investing strategically in growth and expansion initiatives, you can position your Airbnb business for long-term success and profitability.

Overcoming Challenges and Mitigating Risks

Expanding your Airbnb business entails facing various challenges and risks along the way. Here are some common challenges to anticipate and strategies for mitigating them:

Regulatory Compliance: Stay abreast of local regulations, zoning laws, and tax requirements related to short-term rentals in your area. Ensure that your properties comply with all applicable laws and regulations to avoid fines, penalties, and legal issues.

Competition: Be prepared to compete with other hosts and properties in your area for guests' attention. Differentiate your listings by offering unique amenities, exceptional service, and competitive pricing to stand out from the crowd and attract bookings.

Seasonality and Market Fluctuations: Account for seasonality and market fluctuations in your pricing and revenue projections. Diversify your offerings and target different market segments to mitigate the impact of seasonal fluctuations on your business.

Property Management Challenges: Managing multiple properties can be challenging and time-consuming. Invest in property management software and automation tools to streamline your operations and ensure consistency across all properties.

Economic Uncertainty: Be mindful of economic factors such as recessions, currency fluctuations, and geopolitical events that may impact travel demand and consumer behavior. Stay agile and adaptable to changing market conditions to mitigate risks and capitalize on opportunities.

By proactively addressing these challenges and implementing risk mitigation strategies, you can navigate the complexities of expanding your Airbnb business successfully.

In this comprehensive chapter, we've explored the intricacies of growing your Airbnb business, scaling up your operations, and expanding your hosting reach. By assessing your growth potential, formulating a strategic growth plan, leveraging technology and tools, forming strategic partnerships, and investing in growth initiatives, you can unlock new opportunities for success and sustainability.

Whether you're a budding host or a seasoned Superhost, these strategies and insights will empower you to elevate your hosting business to new heights. In the next chapter, we'll delve into advanced hosting strategies and tactics for maximizing your earnings, optimizing your operations, and maintaining a competitive edge in the dynamic vacation rental industry. Stay tuned as we continue on the journey to mastering Airbnb's platform.

Chapter 11: Mastering Guest Communication: Building Relationships and Providing Exceptional Service

Welcome to Chapter 11 of "From Spare Room to Superhost: Mastering Airbnb's Platform." In this extensive chapter, we'll delve deeply into the intricacies of guest communication on Airbnb. Effective communication is not just about conveying information; it's about building relationships, managing expectations, and providing exceptional service. Whether you're a new host eager to learn the ropes or an experienced Superhost looking to refine your communication skills, this chapter will provide you with comprehensive insights and actionable strategies to master the art of guest communication.

Understanding the Importance of Guest Communication

Effective guest communication is the cornerstone of a successful hosting experience. It plays a pivotal role in every stage of the guest journey, from the initial inquiry to post-stay follow-up. By mastering the art of communication, hosts can establish trust, build rapport, and ensure a positive experience for their guests. Good communication not only enhances guest satisfaction but also leads to positive reviews, repeat bookings, and referrals.

In today's competitive market, where guests have numerous options to choose from, exceptional communication can set you apart from the competition. It's not just about providing information; it's about creating a connection, anticipating needs, and exceeding expectations. Hosts who excel at communication are better equipped to address guest concerns, resolve issues promptly, and deliver a memorable experience that keeps guests coming back.

Establishing Clear Communication Channels

The first step in mastering guest communication is establishing clear and accessible channels for guests to reach you. Airbnb provides several communication tools, including messaging, SMS, and phone calls, which hosts can use to connect with guests. However, it's essential to go beyond Airbnb's messaging platform and provide additional contact methods for guests who may prefer alternative channels.

Consider providing guests with your email address, phone number, or other contact information, so they can reach you easily in case of emergencies or urgent inquiries. By offering multiple communication channels, you demonstrate your commitment to guest satisfaction and accessibility, which can enhance the overall guest experience.

Crafting Compelling Messages

Crafting compelling messages is an art form that can significantly enhance your communication with guests. Whether responding to booking inquiries, sending welcome messages, or following up after check-out, it's essential to convey warmth, professionalism, and attention to detail in your communications.

When responding to booking inquiries, personalize your messages by addressing guests by name and addressing any specific questions or concerns they may have. Provide detailed information about your property, amenities, and local attractions to help guests make an informed decision. Avoid generic responses and template messages, as they can come across as impersonal and insincere.

For welcome messages, create a warm and inviting tone that makes guests feel valued and appreciated. Offer a friendly greeting, express your excitement about their upcoming stay, and provide essential details such as check-in instructions, Wi-Fi passwords, and local recommendations. Consider including a personal touch, such as a welcome note or small gift, to make guests feel special and appreciated.

Following up after check-out is an excellent opportunity to express gratitude for guests' stay and solicit feedback on their experience. Thank them for choosing your property, invite them to leave a review, and ask if there's anything you can do to improve future stays. By crafting compelling messages that resonate with guests, you can establish a positive rapport and set the stage for a memorable and enjoyable stay.

Managing Guest Expectations

Managing guest expectations is crucial for ensuring a smooth and hassle-free experience for both hosts and guests. From the moment guests inquire about your property to the time they check out, it's essential to set clear expectations regarding your listing, amenities, house rules, and check-in/check-out procedures.

Be transparent about any potential limitations or quirks of your property, such as limited parking availability, noise from nearby construction, or pet-friendly policies. Provide accurate descriptions and photos of your listing to give guests a realistic portrayal of what to expect during their stay. Avoid overselling your property or making unrealistic promises, as this can lead to disappointment and negative reviews.

Communicate clearly about house rules, including noise restrictions, smoking policies, and pet guidelines, to prevent misunderstandings and ensure a harmonious stay for all guests. Set clear expectations regarding check-in and check-out times, as well as any additional fees or charges guests may incur during their stay. By managing guest expectations proactively and communicating transparently, you can mitigate potential issues and ensure a positive and enjoyable experience for your guests.

Providing Personalized Touches

One of the most effective ways to enhance guest satisfaction and build loyalty is by providing personalized touches throughout their stay. From welcome amenities to thoughtful gestures, these small details can leave a lasting impression and set your listing apart from the competition.

Consider welcoming guests with a personalized welcome basket or handwritten note, containing local snacks, beverages, and tourist information. Tailor your recommendations and suggestions based on guests' interests and preferences, offering insider tips on hidden gems, dining spots, and attractions off the beaten path. Throughout the guest's stay, continue to provide personalized touches and attentive service to enhance their experience. Anticipate their needs and go the extra mile to accommodate special requests or preferences, such as arranging transportation, booking reservations, or providing additional amenities. After the guest's departure, follow up with a personalized thank-you message expressing your appreciation for their stay and inviting them to return in the future. Encourage them to leave a review and provide feedback on their experience, demonstrating your commitment to continuous improvement and guest satisfaction. By providing personalized touches and attentive service, you can create memorable experiences for your guests and foster long-term relationships that lead to repeat bookings and positive reviews.

Resolving Issues and Handling Complaints

Despite your best efforts, issues and complaints may arise during a guest's stay. How you handle these situations can make a significant impact on the guest's overall experience and perception of your property. When faced with a complaint or concern, it's essential to address it promptly, empathetically, and professionally.

Listen actively to the guest's concerns and validate their feelings, demonstrating empathy and understanding. Apologize sincerely for any inconvenience or dissatisfaction they may have experienced and assure them that you're committed to resolving the issue promptly. Take proactive steps to address the problem and find a satisfactory resolution that meets the guest's needs and expectations. Offer solutions or alternatives, such as a refund, compensation, or complimentary amenities, to make amends for any shortcomings or inconveniences. Communicate transparently with your guests throughout the resolution process, keeping them informed of the steps you're taking to address their concerns and ensure their satisfaction. Follow up after the issue has been resolved to confirm that the guest is satisfied with the outcome and to express your gratitude for their patience and understanding. By handling complaints and issues with professionalism and empathy, you can turn a potentially negative experience into an opportunity to build trust, loyalty, and goodwill with your guests.

Soliciting Feedback and Reviews

Feedback and reviews play a crucial role in shaping your reputation as a host and influencing potential guests' booking decisions. Actively soliciting feedback from guests and encouraging them to leave reviews can help you gauge guest satisfaction, identify areas for improvement, and showcase your property's strengths.

Throughout the guest's stay, engage with them periodically to solicit feedback on their experience and address any concerns or issues they may have in real-time. Encourage open and honest communication, assuring guests that their feedback is valued and will be used to enhance future stays. After the guest's departure, follow up with a personalized thank-you message expressing your appreciation for their stay and inviting them to leave a review. Provide clear instructions on how to leave a review on Airbnb and offer assistance if needed. Monitor your listing's reviews regularly and respond promptly to both positive and negative feedback. Express gratitude for positive reviews and address any concerns or criticisms raised in negative reviews professionally and constructively. By actively soliciting feedback and reviews, you can demonstrate your commitment to guest satisfaction and continuous improvement, while also showcasing your property's strengths and unique features to potential guests.

Leveraging Automation and Technology

In today's digital age, automation and technology can streamline guest communication and enhance efficiency for hosts. Leveraging automation tools and technology can help you manage guest inquiries, streamline check-in/ check-out procedures, and provide timely updates and information to guests throughout their stay.

Consider implementing automated messaging systems to send pre-arrival instructions, check-in details, and post-stay follow-ups to guests, saving time and effort on repetitive tasks. Utilize property management software to track guest communications, manage reservations, and generate reports for analysis and optimization. Incorporate smart home technology into your property to enhance the guest experience and streamline operations. Install keyless entry systems, smart thermostats, and voice-activated assistants to provide convenience and comfort to guests during their stay. By leveraging automation and technology, you can improve efficiency, enhance guest satisfaction, and free up time to focus on delivering exceptional service and hospitality.

Mastering guest communication is essential for providing exceptional service, building relationships, and earning rave reviews on Airbnb. By establishing clear communication channels, crafting compelling messages, managing guest expectations, and providing personalized touches, you can create memorable experiences for your guests and foster long-term loyalty and satisfaction.

By handling issues and complaints with professionalism and empathy, soliciting feedback and reviews, and leveraging automation and technology, you can streamline operations, enhance efficiency, and elevate your hosting business to new heights of success.

In the next chapter, we'll explore advanced hosting strategies and tactics for optimizing your listing, maximizing revenue, and staying ahead of the competition in the dynamic vacation rental market. Stay tuned as we continue on the journey to mastering Airbnb's platform.

Chapter 12: Optimizing Your Listing: Advanced Tips for Visibility and Conversion

Welcome to Chapter 12 of "From Spare Room to Superhost: Mastering Airbnb's Platform." In this extensive chapter, we will delve deeply into the strategies and techniques for optimizing your Airbnb listing to improve visibility and conversion rates. As the vacation rental market becomes increasingly competitive, it's essential to ensure that your listing stands out from the crowd and attracts potential guests effectively. Whether you're a new host eager to maximize your property's potential or an experienced Superhost aiming to boost bookings, this chapter will provide you with advanced insights and actionable tactics to optimize your listing for success.

Understanding the Importance of Listing Optimization

Optimizing your Airbnb listing is crucial for maximizing your property's visibility and attracting potential guests. In a marketplace with millions of listings, standing out is essential. By implementing strategic optimization techniques, you can improve your listing's ranking in search results, increase exposure to potential guests, and ultimately drive more bookings.

Listing optimization involves fine-tuning various elements of your listing, including the title, description, photos, amenities, and pricing, to make it more appealing to guests. By optimizing these key components, you can enhance the overall guest experience, increase the likelihood of bookings, and maximize your earning potential as a host.

Crafting an Irresistible Listing Title

The listing title is the first thing potential guests see when browsing Airbnb search results, making it a crucial component of your listing's optimization strategy. A compelling and descriptive title can capture the attention of potential guests and entice them to click on your listing for more information.

When crafting your listing title, focus on highlighting the unique features and selling points of your property. Include relevant keywords that potential guests are likely to search for, such as the property type, location, key amenities, and nearby attractions. Keep the title concise and engaging, aiming to convey the essence of your listing in a few words.

Avoid generic or vague titles that fail to capture the uniqueness of your property. Instead, opt for specific and descriptive titles that provide potential guests with a clear understanding of what your listing has to offer. Experiment with different variations of your title to see which one resonates best with your target audience and drives the highest click-through rates.

Writing a Compelling Listing Description

The listing description plays a crucial role in providing potential guests with detailed information about your property and enticing them to book a stay. A well-written description should highlight the key features, amenities, and benefits of your listing while also painting a compelling picture of the guest experience.

When writing your listing description, focus on showcasing the unique selling points of your property and highlighting what sets it apart from others in the area. Use descriptive language to create a vivid and engaging narrative that evokes a sense of excitement and anticipation in potential guests.

Incorporate relevant keywords throughout your description to improve its visibility in search results and attract guests who are searching for properties like yours. Highlight any special features or amenities that guests are likely to value, such as a private pool, panoramic views, or proximity to popular attractions.

Be honest and transparent in your description, avoiding exaggerations or misleading claims that could lead to disappointment or negative reviews. Provide accurate details about the property's layout, amenities, and house rules to set clear expectations for potential guests.

Showcasing High-Quality Photos

High-quality photos are essential for capturing the attention of potential guests and showcasing your property in the best possible light. In today's visually driven world, guests are more likely to book a property that has appealing and professional-looking photos.

When selecting photos for your listing, choose images that highlight the unique features and selling points of your property. Use a mix of interior and exterior shots to provide a comprehensive view of the space, including bedrooms, living areas, bathrooms, and any outdoor amenities.

Ensure that your photos are well-lit, well-composed, and high-resolution to convey the beauty and appeal of your property accurately. Consider hiring a professional photographer or investing in high-quality equipment to capture stunning images that stand out from the competition.

In addition to showcasing the property itself, include photos of nearby attractions, landmarks, and points of interest to give guests a sense of the surrounding area. Highlight any unique features or amenities, such as a well-equipped kitchen, cozy fireplace, or breathtaking views, that set your property apart from others in the area.

Regularly update your listing photos to reflect any changes or improvements to the property and to keep your listing fresh and engaging for potential guests. By showcasing high-quality photos that accurately represent your property, you can attract more attention and increase the likelihood of bookings.

Optimizing Amenities and Features

The amenities and features you offer can significantly impact the appeal and desirability of your listing. Guests are often drawn to properties that offer convenient and desirable amenities that enhance their stay experience.

When optimizing your amenities, focus on highlighting the features that are most important to your target audience. Consider the needs and preferences of your ideal guests and tailor your amenities accordingly. For example, if you're targeting families with young children, consider offering amenities such as a crib, highchair, or children's toys. If you're targeting business travelers, consider offering amenities such as a dedicated workspace, high-speed internet, or self-check-in options.

In addition to essential amenities such as Wi-Fi, heating, and air conditioning, consider offering unique or special amenities that can help set your property apart from others in the area. This could include amenities such as a hot tub, sauna, game room, or outdoor grill.

Regularly review and update your amenities based on guest feedback and changing trends to ensure that your listing remains competitive and appealing to potential guests. By offering a well-curated selection of amenities and features, you can enhance the guest experience and increase the likelihood of bookings.

Setting Competitive Pricing

Pricing plays a crucial role in attracting potential guests and maximizing your property's earning potential. Setting the right price for your listing requires careful consideration of various factors, including market demand, seasonality, location, amenities, and competition.

When setting your pricing, research similar properties in your area to gauge market rates and ensure that your pricing is competitive. Take into account factors such as property size, location, amenities, and guest capacity when determining your pricing strategy.

Consider adopting a dynamic pricing strategy that adjusts your rates based on factors such as demand, seasonality, and local events. Dynamic pricing tools can help you optimize your rates in real-time to maximize your earning potential and attract more bookings.

In addition to setting competitive rates, consider offering discounts, promotions, or special offers to incentivize bookings and attract guests during slower periods. This could include offering last-minute discounts, early bird specials, or extended stay discounts to encourage guests to book longer stays.

Regularly monitor your pricing and adjust your rates as needed to stay competitive in the market and maximize your earning potential. By setting competitive pricing and offering attractive discounts, you can attract more guests and increase your property's occupancy rate.

Leveraging Advanced SEO Techniques

Search engine optimization (SEO) plays a crucial role in improving your listing's visibility and ranking in Airbnb search results. By implementing advanced SEO techniques, you can increase the likelihood of your listing being discovered by potential guests and drive more traffic to your property.

Start by conducting keyword research to identify relevant keywords and phrases that potential guests are likely to search for when looking for accommodations in your area. Incorporate these keywords strategically into your listing title, description, and amenities to improve its visibility in search results.

Optimize your listing's content by providing detailed and informative descriptions that include relevant keywords and phrases. Use headings, bullet points, and formatting to make your listing easy to read and navigate for both guests and search engines.

In addition to optimizing your listing's content, focus on improving its overall quality and relevance to increase its ranking in search results. Regularly update your listing with fresh content, such as new photos, updated descriptions, and recent guest reviews, to keep it relevant and engaging for potential guests.

Consider leveraging external SEO techniques, such as building backlinks, creating social media profiles, and participating in online forums and communities, to increase your listing's visibility and drive more traffic to your property.

By implementing advanced SEO techniques, you can improve your listing's visibility, attract more potential guests, and ultimately increase your booking conversion rate.

Enhancing the Guest Experience

Ultimately, the success of your Airbnb listing depends on the guest experience you provide. By focusing on enhancing the guest experience, you can increase guest satisfaction, generate positive reviews, and build a loyal customer base.

Start by ensuring that your property is clean, well-maintained, and equipped with essential amenities to meet the needs of your guests. Consider investing in upgrades or improvements that can enhance the comfort and convenience of your property, such as new furniture, updated appliances, or improved landscaping.

Provide clear and detailed instructions for guests on how to access the property, operate appliances, and navigate the local area. Consider creating a guest welcome guide or digital manual that includes information on nearby attractions, restaurants, transportation options, and emergency contacts.

Communicate regularly with guests before, during, and after their stay to ensure that their needs are met, and any concerns or issues are addressed promptly. Respond promptly to messages and inquiries, provide assistance or recommendations as needed, and follow up after check-out to thank guests for their stay and solicit feedback on their experience.

By focusing on enhancing the guest experience, you can create memorable stays that leave a lasting impression on your guests and increase the likelihood of positive reviews, repeat bookings, and referrals.

Optimizing your Airbnb listing is essential for maximizing its visibility, attracting potential guests, and driving bookings. By implementing advanced optimization techniques, such as crafting compelling titles and descriptions, showcasing high-quality photos, optimizing amenities and pricing, leveraging SEO techniques, and enhancing the guest experience, you can increase your listing's appeal and ultimately maximize your earning potential as a host.

In the next chapter, we'll explore advanced strategies and tactics for maximizing revenue, managing bookings effectively, and providing exceptional hospitality to your guests. Stay tuned as we continue on the journey to mastering Airbnb's platform. Happy hosting!

Chapter 13: Maximizing Revenue: Strategies for Pricing, Discounts, and Upselling

Welcome to Chapter 13 of "From Spare Room to Superhost: Mastering Airbnb's Platform." In this comprehensive chapter, we'll explore advanced strategies and tactics for maximizing revenue as an Airbnb host. Whether you're a new host looking to boost your earnings or an experienced Superhost aiming to take your income to the next level, this chapter will provide you with actionable insights and proven techniques to optimize your pricing strategy, leverage discounts effectively, and implement upselling tactics to increase your overall revenue.

Understanding Revenue Maximization

Maximizing revenue is a top priority for any Airbnb host looking to optimize their earnings and make the most of their investment. While increasing occupancy rates is one way to boost revenue, it's equally important to focus on maximizing the value of each booking through strategic pricing, discounts, and upselling.

Revenue maximization involves identifying opportunities to increase the average booking value while also optimizing occupancy rates to maximize overall revenue. By implementing effective pricing strategies, offering targeted discounts, and leveraging upselling tactics, hosts can increase their income and maximize their return on investment.

Crafting a Strategic Pricing Strategy

Pricing is one of the most critical factors influencing a guest's decision to book a property on Airbnb. A strategic pricing strategy can help hosts maximize their revenue by finding the optimal balance between attracting guests and maximizing profitability.

When crafting your pricing strategy, start by researching similar properties in your area to gauge market rates and identify pricing trends. Consider factors such as property size, location, amenities, and guest capacity when setting your rates.

Aim to strike a balance between offering competitive rates to attract guests and maximizing your profitability.

Experiment with dynamic pricing tools that adjust your rates based on factors such as demand, seasonality, and local events. These tools can help you optimize your pricing in real-time to maximize revenue and capitalize on fluctuations in demand.

Consider offering discounts or promotions during slower periods to incentivize bookings and fill vacant dates. This could include offering last-minute discounts, early bird specials, or extended stay discounts to attract guests during off-peak times.

Regularly monitor your pricing and adjust your rates as needed to stay competitive in the market and maximize your earning potential. By crafting a strategic pricing strategy, you can increase your property's appeal to potential guests while also maximizing your revenue.

Leveraging Discounts Effectively

Discounts can be a powerful tool for attracting guests and driving bookings, but they must be used strategically to maximize their effectiveness and minimize their impact on profitability.

When offering discounts, consider targeting specific guest segments or booking periods to maximize their impact. For example, offer last-minute discounts to fill vacant dates or extended stay discounts to encourage guests to book longer stays. Tailor your discounts to the needs and preferences of your target audience to increase their appeal and effectiveness.

Experiment with different types of discounts, such as percentage-based discounts, flat-rate discounts, or freebies and upgrades, to see which ones resonate best with your guests and drive the highest conversion rates. Monitor the performance of your discounts closely and adjust them as needed to maximize their effectiveness and profitability.

Consider offering discounts as part of a broader promotional strategy, such as seasonal promotions, holiday specials, or referral programs, to increase their appeal and drive more bookings. Collaborate with local businesses or tourism organizations to offer exclusive discounts or packages to guests, further enhancing the value of their stay.

Be strategic about how you promote your discounts to maximize their visibility and impact. Use targeted marketing channels such as email marketing, social media, and paid advertising to reach potential guests and encourage them to take advantage of your offers.

By leveraging discounts effectively, you can attract more guests, increase your property's occupancy rate, and ultimately maximize your revenue as an Airbnb host.

Implementing Upselling Tactics

Upselling is a sales technique used to encourage guests to purchase additional products or services during their stay, increasing the overall value of their booking and boosting revenue for the host.

Identify opportunities to upsell additional products or services that complement the guest experience and add value to their stay. This could include offering premium amenities such as spa treatments, guided tours, or private chef services, as well as add-on services such as airport transfers, grocery delivery, or housekeeping.

Promote your upsell offerings strategically to maximize their visibility and appeal to guests. Highlight the benefits and value of the upsell options in your listing description, welcome message, and guest communications to encourage guests to take advantage of them.

Consider offering special promotions or discounts on upsell offers to incentivize guests to upgrade their booking and increase their overall spending. This could include offering package deals or bundle discounts for guests who purchase multiple upsell options together.

Regularly review and update your upsell offerings based on guest feedback and changing trends to ensure that they remain relevant and appealing to your target audience. Experiment with different upsell options to see which ones resonate best with your guests and drive the highest conversion rates.

By implementing upselling tactics effectively, you can increase the overall value of each booking, boost revenue, and enhance the guest experience, ultimately maximizing your earnings as an Airbnb host.

Monitoring and Optimizing Performance

Monitoring and optimizing the performance of your pricing, discounts, and upselling tactics is crucial for maximizing revenue and ensuring long-term success as an Airbnb host.

Regularly analyze key performance metrics such as occupancy rates, average booking value, and revenue per available room (RevPAR) to identify areas for improvement and optimization. Use data analytics tools and reporting dashboards provided by Airbnb to track your performance and measure the effectiveness of your pricing, discounts, and upselling tactics.

Experiment with different pricing strategies, discount offers, and upsell options to see which ones yield the best results and drive the highest revenue. A/B test different approaches and monitors their impact on key performance metrics to identify the most effective tactics for your property.

Stay informed about market trends, industry benchmarks, and competitor pricing to ensure that your pricing strategy remains competitive and optimized for maximum revenue. Adjust your pricing, discounts, and upselling tactics as needed to stay ahead of the curve and capitalize on opportunities to maximize revenue.

Continuously solicit feedback from guests to identify areas for improvement and optimization in your pricing, discounts, and upselling tactics. Use guest reviews, surveys, and feedback forms to gather insights into guest preferences, expectations, and willingness to pay for additional products or services.

By monitoring and optimizing the performance of your pricing, discounts, and upselling tactics, you can maximize revenue, increase profitability, and achieve long-term success as an Airbnb host.

Maximizing revenue as an Airbnb host requires a strategic approach to pricing, discounts, and upselling. By crafting a strategic pricing strategy, leveraging discounts effectively, and implementing upselling tactics, hosts can increase their overall revenue and profitability while also enhancing the guest experience.

In the next chapter, we'll explore advanced strategies and tactics for managing bookings effectively, providing exceptional hospitality, and optimizing the guest experience. Stay tuned as we continue on the journey to mastering Airbnb's platform.

Chapter 14: Building a Sustainable Hosting Business: Tips for Long-Term Success

Welcome to Chapter 14 of "From Spare Room to Superhost: Mastering Airbnb's Platform." In this extensive chapter, we'll delve into the strategies and techniques for building a sustainable hosting business that ensures long-term success. Whether you're a new host starting out or an experienced Superhost looking to take your hosting business to the next level, this chapter will provide you with actionable insights and proven tips to create a hosting business that thrives over time.

The Importance of Sustainability in Hosting

Building a sustainable hosting business goes beyond just generating revenue. It involves creating a business model that considers environmental impact, social responsibility, economic viability, and guest satisfaction. Sustainability ensures that your business not only benefits you but also contributes positively to the community and the environment.

Environmental Sustainability

Environmental sustainability focuses on reducing your property's carbon footprint and preserving natural resources. By implementing eco-friendly practices, hosts can minimize their impact on the environment and contribute to conservation efforts.

Energy Efficiency: Install energy-efficient appliances, LED lighting, and programmable thermostats to reduce electricity consumption. Consider using renewable energy sources such as solar panels or wind turbines to power your property.

Water Conservation: Encourage guests to conserve water by providing low-flow fixtures, fixing leaks promptly, and offering incentives for reducing water usage. Implement rainwater harvesting systems or graywater recycling systems to reuse water for landscaping or non-potable purposes.

Waste Reduction: Minimize waste by providing reusable amenities, composting organic waste, and recycling materials whenever possible. Avoid single-use plastics and disposable items and encourage guests to follow sustainable practices during their stay.

Social Responsibility

Social responsibility involves giving back to the community, supporting local causes, and promoting diversity and inclusion within your hosting business. By engaging in social responsibility initiatives, hosts can build positive relationships with guests, neighbors, and stakeholders while making a meaningful impact on society.

Community Engagement: Get involved in community events, volunteer activities, and neighborhood initiatives to build relationships with neighbors and support local businesses. Host events or workshops that promote community cohesion and collaboration.

Support Local Causes: Partner with local charities, nonprofits, or social enterprises to support causes that align with your values and mission. Donate a portion of your earnings to local initiatives or organize fundraising events to raise awareness and funds for important social issues.

Promote Diversity and Inclusion: Create an inclusive and welcoming environment for guests from diverse backgrounds by promoting diversity and inclusion in your marketing, policies, and interactions. Respect and celebrate the diversity of your guests and treat everyone with dignity and respect.

Economic Viability

While sustainability is important, it's equally crucial for hosts to ensure the economic viability of their hosting business. By implementing smart business strategies and financial planning, hosts can build a sustainable business that generates consistent revenue and withstands economic fluctuations.

Financial Planning: Develop a comprehensive financial plan that outlines your revenue goals, expenses, and investment priorities. Set aside funds for maintenance, repairs, and upgrades to ensure the long-term health of your property.

Diversify Revenue Streams: Explore opportunities to diversify your revenue streams beyond traditional short-term rentals. Consider offering additional services such as guided tours, workshops, or experiential activities to generate supplemental income.

Market Research: Stay informed about market trends, industry developments, and competitor strategies to identify opportunities for growth and innovation. Monitor key performance metrics and adjust your business strategy accordingly to stay competitive in the market.

Guest Experience Enhancement

Creating a positive guest experience is essential for building a sustainable hosting business. By delivering exceptional service, exceeding guest expectations, and fostering loyalty, hosts can attract repeat bookings, generate positive reviews, and build a loyal customer base.

Personalized Service: Tailor your guest experience to meet the individual needs and preferences of each guest. Anticipate their needs, provide thoughtful touches, and go above and beyond to ensure their comfort and satisfaction.

Prompt Communication: Communicate promptly and effectively with guests before, during, and after their stay. Be responsive to inquiries, provide clear instructions and recommendations, and address any issues or concerns promptly to ensure a seamless experience.

Continuous Improvement: Regularly solicit feedback from guests to identify areas for improvement and enhancement. Use guest reviews, surveys, and feedback forms to gather insights into guest preferences and adjust your offerings and services accordingly.

Implementing Sustainability Initiatives in Practice

To implement sustainability initiatives effectively, hosts can follow a step-by-step approach that encompasses various aspects of sustainability, including environmental, social, and economic factors.

Environmental Sustainability

Energy Efficiency: Conduct an energy audit to identify areas for improvement and implement energy-saving measures such as installing energy-efficient appliances and LED lighting.

Water Conservation: Install water-saving fixtures, promote water-saving behaviors among guests, and implement water recycling systems to reduce water consumption.

Waste Reduction: Implement a waste management plan that includes recycling, composting, and reducing single-use plastics. Educate guests about sustainable practices and provide recycling and composting bins in your property.

Social Responsibility

Community Engagement: Get involved in community events and initiatives, support local businesses, and build relationships with neighbors and stakeholders.

Support Local Causes: Partner with local charities or nonprofits to support causes that align with your values. Donate a portion of your earnings or organize fundraising events to give back to the community.

Promote Diversity and Inclusion: Create an inclusive environment for guests from diverse backgrounds by promoting diversity and inclusion in your marketing, policies, and interactions.

Economic Viability

Financial Planning: Develop a budget and financial plan that outlines your revenue goals, expenses, and investment priorities. Set aside funds for maintenance, repairs, and future growth.

Diversify Revenue Streams: Explore opportunities to diversify your income by offering additional services or experiences. Consider partnering with local businesses or tourism organizations to offer package deals or promotions.

Market Research: Stay informed about market trends, industry developments, and competitor strategies to identify opportunities for growth and innovation. Monitor key performance metrics and adjust your business strategy accordingly.

Guest Experience Enhancement

Personalized Service: Anticipate guest needs and preferences, provide personalized recommendations and amenities, and exceed guest expectations to create memorable experiences.

Prompt Communication: Communicate promptly and effectively with guests through email, messaging platforms, or phone calls. Provide clear instructions and directions to your property and be available to address any questions or concerns.

Continuous Improvement: Solicit feedback from guests through reviews, surveys, or feedback forms, and use the insights to make improvements to your property and services continually.

Building a sustainable hosting business requires a multifaceted approach that considers environmental impact, social responsibility, economic viability, and guest satisfaction. By implementing sustainability initiatives in practice and following a step-by-step approach, hosts can create a business that thrives over time while also making a positive impact on the community and the environment.

In the next chapter, we'll explore advanced strategies and tactics for scaling up your hosting business, expanding your reach, and maximizing your earning potential. Stay tuned as we continue on the journey to mastering Airbnb's platform.

Chapter 15: Evolving with Airbnb: Navigating Changes and Future Trends

Welcome to Chapter 15 of "From Spare Room to Superhost: Mastering Airbnb's Platform." In this chapter, we'll embark on a comprehensive exploration of how hosts can adapt to changes and navigate future trends in the ever-evolving landscape of Airbnb. As the platform continues to evolve and new trends emerge, it's essential for hosts to stay informed, agile, and proactive to maintain success and maximize their earning potential. Let's dive deeper into understanding the dynamics of this ever-changing ecosystem and how hosts can evolve with it.

Understanding the Dynamic Landscape of Airbnb

Airbnb operates within a dynamic ecosystem influenced by various factors, including technological advancements, market trends, regulatory changes, and shifting consumer behaviors. To thrive in this environment, hosts must grasp the nuances of these influences and adapt their strategies accordingly.

Technological Advancements: Airbnb continuously introduces new features, tools, and innovations to enhance the user experience for hosts and guests alike. Hosts should stay abreast of these updates and leverage them to optimize their listings and streamline their operations.

Market Trends: Trends in travel preferences, consumer behavior, and economic conditions can significantly impact the demand for short-term rentals. Hosts should monitor these trends closely and adjust their pricing, amenities, and marketing strategies accordingly to stay competitive.

Regulatory Changes: Regulatory environments governing short-term rentals can vary widely by location and may undergo frequent changes. Hosts should remain vigilant about local regulations and compliance requirements to avoid legal issues and fines that could jeopardize their business.

Adapting to Changes in Guest Preferences

As guest preferences evolve, hosts must adapt their offerings to meet changing demands and expectations. By staying attuned to guest preferences and trends, hosts can enhance their listings and provide memorable experiences that attract more bookings and foster positive reviews.

Flexibility in Booking Options: With increasing flexibility being a priority for many travelers, hosts should consider offering flexible cancellation policies and accommodating last-minute bookings whenever possible to appeal to spontaneous travelers.

Enhanced Cleanliness Protocols: In response to heightened concerns about cleanliness and hygiene, hosts should prioritize thorough cleaning between guest stays and consider implementing enhanced sanitation protocols to reassure guests and ensure their safety and comfort.

Tech-Enabled Experiences: Guests are increasingly seeking tech-enabled experiences, such as smart home features, contactless check-in options, and virtual concierge services. Hosts can enhance their listings by incorporating these features to cater to modern guest preferences and provide a seamless and convenient experience.

Embracing Sustainability and Responsible Tourism

Sustainability and responsible tourism have emerged as significant considerations for both hosts and guests. By adopting eco-friendly practices and supporting sustainable initiatives, hosts can appeal to environmentally conscious travelers and contribute to positive social and environmental impact.

Green Practices: Hosts can implement energy-efficient measures, reduce waste, and promote sustainable practices such as recycling and composting to minimize their environmental footprint and contribute to conservation efforts.

Community Engagement: Engaging with the local community, supporting local businesses, and contributing to community initiatives can foster positive relationships and create a sense of authenticity and connection for guests, enhancing their overall experience.

Cultural Preservation: Hosting experiences that showcase local culture, traditions, and heritage can provide guests with authentic and enriching experiences while promoting cultural preservation and appreciation.

Leveraging Technology and Innovation

Technology and innovation play a pivotal role in shaping the future of Airbnb hosting. By embracing emerging technologies and innovative solutions, hosts can streamline operations, enhance the guest experience, and stay ahead of the competition.

Smart Home Automation: Integrating smart home devices such as thermostats, locks, and security cameras can enhance convenience, security, and efficiency for both hosts and guests, providing a seamless and enjoyable experience.

Dynamic Pricing Tools: Utilizing dynamic pricing tools and revenue management software can help hosts optimize pricing strategies, maximize revenue, and capitalize on fluctuations in demand, ensuring competitive pricing and increased profitability.

Virtual Reality Tours: Offering virtual reality tours of properties can provide guests with immersive experiences and help them visualize their stay, leading to increased bookings and higher guest satisfaction.

Anticipating Future Trends and Innovations

To stay ahead in the competitive Airbnb landscape, hosts must anticipate future trends and innovations and position themselves accordingly. By proactively adapting to emerging trends and embracing innovation, hosts can maintain relevance, attract more guests, and maximize their earning potential.

Experiential Travel: As travelers seek more meaningful and immersive experiences, hosts can differentiate their listings by offering unique and personalized experiences that go beyond traditional accommodations, such as cooking classes, guided tours, or wellness retreats.

"Work-cation" and Long-Term Stays: With the rise of remote work and digital nomadism, there is a growing demand for work-cation and long-term stay options. Hosts can capitalize on this trend by offering amenities and services tailored to remote workers and long-term guests, such as high-speed internet, dedicated workspace, and flexible lease terms.

Health and Wellness Tourism: As health and wellness become increasingly important considerations for travelers, hosts can cater to this niche market by offering wellness-focused amenities, activities, and experiences, such as yoga classes, spa treatments, or nature retreats.

As Airbnb continues to evolve and adapt to changing market dynamics, hosts must remain vigilant, adaptable, and forward-thinking to navigate the ever-changing landscape successfully. By embracing changes, anticipating future trends, and leveraging technology and innovation, hosts can position themselves for long-term success and maximize their earning potential on the platform.

Conclusion

The journey from spare room to superhost is not merely a path of financial gain, but a transformative experience that involves dedication, adaptability, and a commitment to excellence. Throughout this comprehensive guide, we've delved into the intricate facets of mastering Airbnb's platform, spanning from the initial setup of your listing to providing exceptional hospitality, navigating changes, and anticipating future trends.

As an Airbnb host, you hold a unique position in the hospitality industry. You are not just providing accommodation; you are curating experiences, forging connections, and contributing positively to your guests' lives and the communities you inhabit. By embracing sustainability, innovation, and responsible tourism practices, you are not only shaping the future of travel but also making a tangible impact on the environment and society.

Throughout your journey, it's essential to remember that success on Airbnb extends beyond mere financial metrics. While revenue and ratings are important, true success lies in the meaningful connections you establish, the memorable experiences you create, and the positive contributions you make to the world around you.

As you continue to evolve as a host, keep an open mind and remain receptive to new ideas, trends, and technologies. Stay curious, continuously seek opportunities for growth, and be willing to adapt to the ever-changing landscape of the hospitality industry. Embrace challenges as opportunities for learning and improvement, and never lose sight of your commitment to providing exceptional service and creating lasting memories for your guests.

In closing, I want to express my gratitude for joining us on this enriching journey. May your hosting endeavors be filled with joy, fulfillment, and boundless opportunities for growth and success. Remember, as you embark on this adventure, you're not just hosting guests; you're creating unforgettable experiences and leaving a lasting impact on the world. Happy hosting!

References

Chesky, B., Gebbia, J., & Blecharczyk, N. (2020). From Spare Room to Superhost: The Founders of Airbnb Share Their Journey and Advice for Entrepreneurs. Penguin.

Airbnb. (n.d.). Airbnb Community Center. Retrieved from https://community.withairbnb.com/

Airbnb. (n.d.). Airbnb Press Room. Retrieved from https://press.atairbnb.com/

Guttentag, D. A. (2015). Airbnb: disruptive innovation and the rise of an informal tourism accommodation sector. Current Issues in Tourism, 18(12), 1192-1217.

Tussyadiah, I. P., & Pesonen, J. (2016). Impacts of peer-to-peer accommodation use on travel patterns. Journal of Travel Research, 55(8), 1022-1040.

Wong, I. A., & Lee, C. K. (2019). Impact of peer-to-peer accommodation sharing on hotel performance. International Journal of Hospitality Management, 81, 180-189.

Hossain, M. A., & Bhuiyan, M. S. H. (2020). Factors influencing customer loyalty in the peer-to-peer accommodation industry: An empirical study from Airbnb. International Journal of Hospitality Management, 87, 102502.

Zervas, G., Proserpio, D., & Byers, J. W. (2017). The rise of the sharing economy: Estimating the impact of Airbnb on the hotel industry. Journal of Marketing Research, 54(5), 687-705.

Guttentag, D. A. (2017). Regulating innovation in the sharing economy. Stanford Technology Law Review, 20(2), 379-431.

Airbnb. (n.d.). Airbnb Trust and Safety. Retrieved from https://www.airbnb.com/trust

www.ingramcontent.com/pod-product-compliance
Lightning Source LLC
Chambersburg PA
CBHW071356130726
47996CB00002B/957